Recollections of a Holocaust Survivor Guided and Saved by Angels

Henry Glick

ISBN: 1450573592
ISBN-13: 9781450573597

Preface

My father began writing his memoirs shortly after his retirement from the Veterans Administration Hospital in Brooklyn, New York where he worked as an engineering draftsman for many years. The idea of writing his memoirs was suggested to him by Madeleine Glick, his daughter-in-law, to whom all its readers owe a debt of gratitude. He worked carefully and conscientiously on the manuscript for several years, consulting a multi-volume English-Russian dictionary when unsure of terms. Although he had an ear for languages and was fluent in several, English was not his native tongue and the text shows signs of this. I have, however, kept the original language to retain the authenticity of his voice and character, limiting edits from the original hand-written draft to corrections of spelling and occasional punctuation. The aim of publishing this work is that, in addition to its interest to family members and friends, it may be of interest to a larger community, expressing as it does, in a very direct and personal way, the fate of an individual life caught in the violent and turbulent vortex of the Second World War.

Boris Glick

Table of Contents

A Brief Family Background

My grandparents lived in Sniatyn, a small town in Galicia, Poland, which at that time was part of the Austro-Hungarian Empire. Hardship forced my grandfather to find another place where he could earn a better living. He decided to emigrate to America. He left by himself, leaving his wife with a small daughter home, promising to bring them over when he found a job and settled down.

Time passed, correspondence stopped, the promise was not fulfilled. Grandma knew that he lived in New York, and decided to go after him to find out what happened. She left for New York with her little five-year old daughter, and found him married to another woman. All efforts at reconciliation were unsuccessful. It was a tragic disappointment for my grandmother and her daughter, my future mother. Having no other choice, they returned back home to Sniatyn. The little girl grew up, met a young man from Bukovina, Rumania, my future father. They got married in 1906.

In 1914 when the First World War began, my mother had four children, three daughters and one son. While the war was raging, our little town Sniatyn went, back and forth, from the hands of one side into those of the other, from the Germans to the Russians and vice versa. When the Russian Cossacks took over the town once again, the Jews were the scapegoats to release their anger for all the setbacks they had suffered on the front. One early Friday morning in July 1915, a mob of horse mounted troopers were let loose by their commanding officers and pillaged the Jewish Quarters of the town, They beat up men, raped women, robbed valuables and food. Our house was among others also rampaged. My mother was pregnant at that time, so when one of them burst in my Father tried to stop him. He got hit with the butt of a rifle on the forehead, blood spilling over his face. They left only after they cleaned the house out of the freshly baked breads, challahs and other baked goods prepared for the Sabbath and the whole week.

A few days later the Jews were ordered to leave their dwellings and assemble on the square next to the Town Hall, just with small packages of first necessities, with no reason why. Whoever will disobey the order, will be shot. They obeyed and did assemble. From there, horse-mounted troopers formed a long column of evicted families from their own homes, old and young with children and infants, expelling and escorting them to the main road, out of town with no destination given. The journey was dragging on for five days and caused a lot of suffering and sickness. When the column entered Chartkov, a town on the Russian border, an order came to stop and settle down. They stayed there for two years and only those who endured the whole ordeal, gradually started to return back home to Sniatyn, among them my parents with the whole family, including my grandma. We had three new additions to our family before I was born, a brother and two sisters. When I was born, I was the eighth in sequence. Later on another brother and sister were born. So we became ten children, four brothers and six sisters.

A Day in My Childhood

We owned a house and mechanical shop. My father was a hard-working, industrious man and good provider; nevertheless, to feed and dress a family of our size was not so easy. Later on we got some help from our two older brothers, but it was not always enough to meet ends. There were times I used to go to school without having breakfast. The school I attended was nearby, so sometimes I used to run home during the long fifteen minute break, to pick up a sandwich. Occasionally my Grandma used to bring it to school. I still remember that even, barely audible knock on the door, while the class was in session, then her slowly emerging head covered with a kerchief, that round, wrinkled face, two smiley shiny eyes, and grey curls covering her forehead, coming through the door opening. I got a sign from the teacher to meet my Grandma. A little bit embarrassed I went to the door, where I was met with a modestly happy smile, picked up the sandwich and not saying thank you I quickly returned to my seat. I felt sorry for not being grateful to Grandma; there was a little reason, but not good enough not to be grateful to her. Two things happened in the preceding break, I was hit with a belt buckle painfully over the head during a fight between kids, where I was just a bystander, then the bell rang, everybody hurried back to classes, so did I. The minute I walked in, another rowdy kid ran into me and hit me with his fist in the stomach. I bent down and couldn't catch my breath for a while. The teacher came in; everybody was in place but me. The pupils stood up and greeted the teacher with the required official greeting. "Blessed shall be the Lord." He made a sign to the class to *sit* down, and turned to me: "Why aren't you in your seat?" I was holding my hands around the upper part of my stomach, in pain and anger, looking at him. Finally, slowly catching my breath, I told him that I got hit in my heart. His face grinned. That is not the heart; he replied and started laughing very loudly. The pupils picked up his laugher and the class went wild. I still can see the mean, sarcastic appearance on his face. I went back quietly to my seat. It just wasn't my day.

The Rebbicyn

Usually, after regular school, I attended a private Hebrew School in the afternoon, twice a week. It was expensive for us, but my parents had great pride in me and they didn't spare any effort to enroll me in it. We studied Hebrew there, reading and writing. On one early spring day, I went to school. The snow was still on the ground but slightly melting. My shoes were a little bit worn out, so by the time I arrived my feet were wet and cold, but it was warm and cosy inside, I took of my coat, sat in a row with other kids The rabbi handed over our previously checked homework and the lesson began, My feet started to warm up, it was a very pleasant relief, but not for long, Suddenly, the door leading to the living quarters burst wide open, the rabbi's wife appeared in the door opening with a red frown on her face, looked around, glanced at me, and pointing her little fat forefinger at me, shouted, "You, Glick, go home, home" she kept repeating and trying to approach me, but was blocked by the rabbi with his body and both hands begging her to calm down, pleading with her: "Please, Mamciu, please!" But it did not work. She kept on advancing towards me, pointing her forefinger and shouting "Out! Out!" I was terribly embarrassed, lost, and for a moment didn't know what to do—obey her order, or talk to the Rabbi and find out what it was all about? But she didn't let me decide, she kept on screaming and chasing me out. I realized that the payments were overdue; I quickly got up, picked up my coat and ran out feeling the compassion and curious eyes from the kids following my departure. I cried a little bit on my way home, but the feeling of indignation and outrage at the way the "rebbicyn" handled the case overcame the other feeling. That incident left a lot of resentment in me, and it was much worse than the case with the teacher in Public School who made fun of me in front of the class, it also affected my life later on.

The Hike

In my early teens, I was a member of a Zionist Youth Organization, "Shomer." We had gatherings, meetings, tea parties, dances, and hikes to the nearby woods in the summer, and trips to summer camps. Those were very happy days in my early teen life. I still remember some of our" adventures" that still remain in my memory, and one was a hike to a neighboring town, Zablotow, twenty-one kilometers away, Two of my friends and myself decided for this venture, We also decided not to tell our parents, because we knew we would never get permission for it.

On the next Sunday, sometime in the middle of July, we met near the house of one of my friends, telling our parents that we were going to the park, and left. As we left the outskirts of our town we took the main road, gravel paved, which connected the two towns. We walked for about two hours, the road was empty, not a living soul, we got a little bit tired and scared. We rested from time to time on the side of the road and realized that we did not plan the hike properly: no food, no water, and no money. It was a hot day; we rested again, keeping our feet up and heads down. We decided not to give up and to continue our hike, after all, the idea of the hike was a test of our endurance, and we approached the town of our destination by sundown.

Finally, we found ourselves in the organization club. We received a very warm and friendly reception. The problem was that we were tired and hungry. But nobody gave a thought about it, and we did not ask for anything. It was getting late; luckily there was a train station nearby the town. Someone, one of the leaders, accompanied us to it, bought tickets and sent us back. It looked like our hike would end happily, but that was not the case. The train station was four kilometers away from our town. The arriving passengers usually commuted to the town with coaches driven by horses. When we arrived, a coachman met us, he pointed with his finger to my friends saying, "you and you come with me," and pointing his finger to me he said, "You go to hell." For a moment I remained in place "frozen." astounded, disappointed, not believing what I heard. I calmed down quickly realizing that it was very late, almost midnight, no more coaches, no money. I ran over to the departing coach, grabbed on to the crossbars in the back and hung on to them. The Coachman noticed me and started to hit me with his whip, while my "friends" were laughing. I was hanging on in that position for about thirty to forty minutes until we approached the outskirts of the town. I jumped off with pain all over my body; the coach quickly disappeared in the darkness. I walked the remaining distance home. I did find real friends, at home, where I was met with great relief, warmth and happiness.

My First Attempt to Earn Some Money

The place where I lived was a small regional town in the south of Poland, near the Romanian border. Twice a week, on Wednesdays and Fridays we had fairs. Farmers from the nearby villages, and Guzuls from the Carpathian Mountains, used to come to town with horse drawn wagons with their farming produce, hand-made goods out of wood, and small bundles of chopped wood for fuel.

Our marketplace—a big square, partially paved with cobble stones, was located in the middle of the town alongside the main street and surrounded with a variety of stores, shops, bars and one pharmacy. In the center, a mall-like structure with a glass roof was erected for markets of meat, poultry, fresh vegetables and fruits. The sides and the back of the structure were used for parking the horse-drawn wagons. The front of the square was enclosed with merchant stands, where a variety of consumer goods and clothing were sold. The place was crowded and noisy

One of my friend's families owned such a stand. I asked him whether they would need help in busy fair days. His father okayed my request. On the next fair day I showed up for work. My job was to walk around through the market square with a carton supported by a band around my neck, filled with small items of consumer goods and sell them to farmers and shoppers. I also had to call out loudly my merchandise with a rhyming verse, to attract customers. I listened carefully to the instructions, not asking any questions, disappeared into the crowd, and started to try to do the selling just the way I was instructed; zigzagging from the sidewalk near stores and shops to the wagons, singing my selling verse to shoppers and farmers. I circled the area back and forth, and lost count of how many times, trying to sell something, but in vain. Apparently my merchandise and my convincing singing verses were of no interest to anyone present. It was not my lucky day.

Late in the afternoon, exhausted and hungry, I returned to the stand and handed over the carton with the untouched merchandise. That's how my first attempt to earn some money ended in failure.

My Second Attempt

One of the neighbors who lived next to our house was a baker. He lived with his wife, they had no children. His specialty was home made bread and pastry. Very often he used to send me to buy groceries, for which I got a treat of pastry. He had a small four wheel carriage, with a shiny white enamel finish, in which he used to make deliveries to the wealthier customers. I knew he had a hernia, so I offered him my help, hoping to make some money, he agreed. I was up early in the morning loading the freshly baked loaves of bread into the carriage. Then I was pulling and he was pushing it all over our little town. By noon time we were back home. As a reward I got another piece of pastry. I did not say a word, assuming that by the end of the week he would give me some money.

The next day he asked me to help him carry a basket of pastry and rolls to the other market place, which was located on the northern edge of our town, where livestock was being bought, sold and traded. It was an early spring day with melting snow still on the ground, and my shoes were not in such good shape, but I agreed and went with him carrying a basket, he carried two. When we arrived there, the place was crowded. We walked around and sold out all the baking goods in the early afternoon, and went home. To my great disappointment, there was no pay this time either

The Price of Naïveté

I enjoyed very much being a member of our youth organization. We had a variety of activities, a lot of fun which brings back pleasant memories. But there are also regrettable adventures invented by one of my friends, who managed to talk me into a stupid idea that smeared those pleasant memories. The idea was to hide away our organization trumpet for a while, just for the fun of it, and then return it. We took the trumpet on an early afternoon in the middle of the week, when nobody was around, and left. We hid it. I must admit that I felt very sorry right away, but it was too late. The next week when we came back to the club we found the members and the leaders puzzled and outraged. It turned out to be a very unpleasant, mean trick. We realized it and admitted that we did it. We returned the trumpet, apologized and asked for forgiveness. As a punishment, we were prohibited from attending the club for four weeks. For me the punishment was double, I was excluded from a partially subsidized trip to a summer camp.

Our Pre-War Family Life

In the late thirties, my older brother Menasha and two of my sisters Anna and Lotte got married. They moved out and started their own families. Although they were all love marriages, the marriage of my oldest brother was preceded by a dramatic event I witnessed, an attempt at suicide.

His girl friend lived in an Ukranian neighborhood. One evening he walked her home from a party. On his way home, he was attacked by a band of hooligans and was badly beaten up; he barely made his way back home. Our Mother was very upset and scared. It took him a while to recover. One day while he was working in our shop, I was around watching him; our Mom walked in and started a conversation carefully, trying to explain to him that the girl he is dating is not the right match. He did not give in, replying heatedly that he loves her and that he is not going to break up the dating. Mom kept on insisting. His anger reached its peak, his lost control, grabbed a bottle of hydrochloric acid on a nearby bench, trying to open the cap and drink it, but fortunately he couldn't. We rushed towards him, grabbed his hands trying to take away the bottle, and we succeeded. Mom was hysterical, but calmed down, crying a lot, and calming him down, she promised not to interfere anymore. By the end of the same year, they got married. It was a very nice wedding, in a rented hall. I still remember it clearly. It was a happy occasion for all of us, especially for me.

I reached thirteen years of age, my bar mitzvah birthday. One of my sisters prepared for me a small blue velvet bag for the phylacteries with an embroidered Star of David in golden silk thread. On my bar mitzvah date, my Father and myself went to the early morning service to our Synagogue. After the prayers, we served liqueur and cake for the present worshipers. Later in the day, all the family celebrated my bar mitzvah with me.

For a while everything appeared to be nice and okay in our family. But not for long. Another of my sisters, Brana, the second in sequential order, worked in a neighboring town. She met a young man, fell in love, but it didn't work out for some reason. She couldn't endure it, took it close to her heart, became ill, got a stroke, and the right side of her body was paralyzed, a misfortune we did not need. She was bed-ridden all that time till I left home one week after the war broke out, July 30th, 1941.

Beginning of World War II

In the late thirties, a non-aggression pact was concluded and signed between the Soviet Union and Nazi Germany by the foreign ministers of the two countries, Molotov and Ribbentrop, an event which astounded the whole world. People could not believe it, but it did happen.

Later on the world also found out, that the pact included the division of Poland between the two powers, the occupation of almost all Western Europe by the Nazis, the annexation of the pre-Baltic States: Lithuania, Latvia and Estonia, parts of Romania, Bessarabia and Bukhovina by the Soviet Union.

In September 1939 the results of the pact started to unfold, a war between Poland and Germany started. The Nazis invaded and captured the western half of Poland and stopped there. It was a short, bloody war, with a lot of destruction and killing that lasted four weeks. The intact remainder of the Polish army retreated to Romania, through our town Sniatyn, which bordered Romania, and from there they went to England.

The Soviet Army did not wait and according to the concluded pact, moved in from the East and invaded the Eastern half of Poland. They called this action" the liberation of Western Ukraine, who needed our brotherly hand of help." Noise and the roar of heavy armor woke up our town the next morning. Red Army units entered with infantry, anti-aircraft artillery, horse-drawn artillery, tractor drawn heavy and long-range artillery, field kitchens, medical units, and a lot of other items which I didn't recognize. The roar and noise lasted for a number of days until all units were stationed in, around, and out of town, close to the Romanian border. Afterward things quieted; there was no visible change in the life in our town for a while, except soldiers marching to and from their barracks singing songs.

Then the new authorities appointed some local people as liaisons through whom they organized meetings with the population, gave new orders and organized election of local government. What became very noticeable is the disappearance of merchandise and produce from the stores. Though our town was a little one, it had a lot of stores, shops, always full of consumer goods and food, no shortages. Very quickly Soviet military personnel cleaned out all stores, paying with worthless rubles; the Polish zloty was out of circulation. Soon the food stores had big lines, consumer goods completely disappeared. There were no supplies or deliveries. It became very hard to get by and feed a family. To make up for it, they entertained us with demonstrations of revolutionary movies, musical concerts in parks, under open skies and indoors. In general, the treatment of the population was friendly, but not for everybody. Suddenly a number of entire families disappeared. These were owners of big stores or enterprises, landlords, land owners, country estate owners, businessmen, so called "unreliables." They were raided and arrested during the nights and taken away, nobody knew where, on short notice, they were permitted to take with themselves only small items of necessities. Houses with the rest of their belongings were sealed and later confiscated.

Medicine for my Third Sister

Very soon, the Red Army continued their drive into northern parts of Romania and annexed the provinces of Bukovina and Bessarabia, areas between the rivers Pimt and Dniester, but they kept the borders between what used to be Poland and Romania, closed. In the meantime, another of my sisters, Sheindel, became ill. The medicine she needed was not available in the two existing pharmacies of our town. We had relatives, an uncle, aunt and their families in the city of Gernowitze, which happens to be on the Romanian side. So we decided to try the pharmacies over there. Since regular commuting was forbidden, we had to find other ways to get there. Because of the existing shortages, some fearless people started to cross the borders illegally to get things. We got in touch with a person who had that experience. I asked my mother to let me go. It was risky; she was afraid and unsure but finally decided to let me go. I met with this person a few days before the crossing, his name was Zysia. He explained to me in detail how we will do it. There was a neighboring village about three miles away where the river Prot, the border line, flowed by with no border post present. We had to be at the crossing point at dawn. At an assigned spot, a village guide with whom Zysia made the arrangements was to meet us and lead us to an area where the water was shallow. On the other side, a railroad station was just a few miles away. From there we could take the train to Gernowitze. The next day after the meeting I was up at three o'clock in the morning, dressed lightly and left with the blessing of my mother. Zysie was waiting for me outside already. It was the beginning of July, a very warm morning.

We went briskly to the village, to the house of the guide. He was a typical, Ukrainian peasant, dressed nationally, with a pleasant appearance. Zysia talked with him for a while, then we left, we walked through a wheat field road to a bushy area close to the river; we sat down. The guide moved out in front, looked around, and then gave us a sign to follow him. We did not manage to make a few steps, when we heard a loud shout: "halt or we shoot!" We stopped, and noticed two tall border guards with sub-machine guns and a dog approaching us. One of them searched us; the other kept an eye on us. Not finding anything they stated that we were violating existing rules by being in a forbidden frontier zone, arrested us and escorted us to the main frontier post in the town.

We were held and interrogated for the rest of the day. Finally, they believed my reason for trying to cross the border and after a lengthy lecture of an hour to obey orders and rules of the new authorities, they released us. My mother was very happy to have me back home. It didn't work, but at least we tried. As time went by, the condition of my ill sister became worse. In spite of all our efforts accessible to us we could not save her. She died prematurely, at the age of twenty-one; it was a great loss to all of us.

Later in the month a call up for military service was ordered by the military registration and enlistment office for all young men twenty to twenty-three. It was only a little bit over half a year of the new Soviet State rule, but they considered us automatically obligated for military duty. Thus one of my brothers was drafted and enlisted, another thing we least needed considering his financial support to our family. My oldest brother was twenty-nine and was not subject for enlistment. He was happily married, they had a beautiful little baby boy, I used to play with him a lot while baby sitting. Two brothers and three sisters remained in our household at that moment.

Entrance for the Gymnasium

The summer of 1940 was almost over, during which a friend and I studied and prepared ourselves for Gymnasium entrance exams. The educational system at the moment remained the same, the official language was still Polish, and more importantly, the gymnasium was free of tuition. I passed the exams and was accepted to the second grade, which was equivalent to the seventh grade of Soviet High School. Outside I was met and congratulated by a group of close friends, one of them my girl friend from our youth organization on which I had my first youthful love crush. We sat for a while on a bench outside the school, and then we strolled a little bit until we were left by ourselves, continuing the stroll holding hands in silence. The time went by so fast, that we didn't notice that we approached the town's park. We sat again on a bench still holding hands. She broke the silence sharing with me her fearful thoughts, that I will meet other girls, and forget her. I calmed her down assuring her that this will never happen. Her fears were based on the fact that she attended another, all-girls school and because of that we wouldn't be able to see each other very often. We embraced each other and kissed each other affectionately; it was a mutual, very happy feeling for both of us. It was our first kiss and we kept sitting embraced for a while not realizing that it was getting late. We left the place holding hands and slowly walking, we approached her house. We embraced and kissed each other before parting, arranging our next meeting near the town's movie theatre. Of course we were too young for anything serious, besides, the turn of events changed all our dreams and hopes. We did meet a few times only during the remaining ten months, before the war started on June 22, 1941 when Nazi Germany invaded the Soviet Union.

The Disaster:
The Nazi-German Invasion
of the Soviet Union

It was a very warm and quiet evening on June 21, 1941. We were watching a movie in the town's park under the open sky, shown to us by the military units stationed in our town. Suddenly we heard calls in anxious voices addressed to the present military personnel to report immediately to their units. In a few minutes, all military men cleared out, the movie demonstration stopped, the remaining viewers also left. We felt something very important happened and that it was not a training alarm. We found out all right, early in the morning, listening to the town's loud speaker, we heard the following: Nazi Germany treacherously assaulted all our western borders from North to South with a surprise army attack and that fierce fighting is raging. Our valiant troops are putting up heroic resistance inflicting heavy casualties on the fascist invaders."

We also found out that numerous industrial cities; among them the capital of the Ukraine, Kiev, had been air-raided and heavily bombed. Our town was embraced with fear. The next day a very big number of bombers flew over our town eastwards, at a high altitude, probably for another air-raid. That event created a panic, people ran to the outskirts of town for safety. On the same day a general mobilization was announced for all able-bodied men from twenty-five to forty. This time the turn came for my oldest married brother, and the husbands of my two older married sisters. They were inducted, given uniforms in the town's assembly point, and sent away to a formation unit. We were never to see them again. Later in the week rumors started to float around from one to another, about brutalities inflicted to the Jewish population. Unfortunately, not everyone believed in these rumors. Shortly after, an official order was issued by authorities to government establishments, cooperative enterprises, stores and warehouses to pack up and leave. Horse drawn wagons were requisitioned for transportation. Most of the employees of these establishments also left. There was advice, but no requirement for the general population to evacuate, but a lot of them did, at their own risk, on foot, mostly Jews, followed by a feeling of uncertainty. It was just the beginning of the war; nobody had the experience or an imagination of the inhuman behavior and atrocities committed by the Nazis later on. We had only one Russian newspaper, few could read. Very few people owned radios; the only place for some information was the loudspeaker in the middle of the town, which was not always on. One of my friends who met me in the town listening to the loudspeaker, urged me to leave together with him since his brothers had also been drafted. I mentioned my girlfriend and asked him to go with me to her house to find out about her intentions. To our surprise, the door was locked and nobody was home. In the evening I discussed my intention to leave with my parents. My mother was crying and gave me no answer. There was no way for all of us to leave. We were eight people, my Grandmother, Father, Mother, our ill and paralyzed sister, my eighteen year-old sister, my younger brother and younger sister six years of age. We would definitely need transportation, but we had no means for it, and nowhere to get it. On the eighth day of the war, June 30, 1941, early in the morning my friend knocked on our window. We were all still sleeping. He told us that people were leaving and urged us to hurry up if we intend to go. I got dressed, so did my sister Sarah and my younger brother Meyer. My parents decided that all three of us should leave. Two bags, one with food and the other with clothing were already packed. We left the house accompanied by our Mother to the outskirts of the town. She cried before parting, embraced and kissed us saying good-bye and wishing us good luck, then walking slowly against the crowd of people leaving, she returned back home.

The Journey

Soon a neighboring girlfriend of my sister joined us. We were still in the town walking on the sidewalk when a heavy-set man approached us and started to persuade us, shouting in a loud voice, urging us to turn back and not worry, that everything would be alright and return to normal when the front line moves away from the town. We did not give in to his persuasion and continued to go ahead. All of a sudden I noticed that my sister and her girlfriend were lagging behind. I asked them not to lag because we could lose each other. They surprised me with a statement that they had decided to return back home. I tried to talk them out of it, but it did not work and they returned. We walked over with my brother to the side of the busy road joining a large number of people walking on foot, among them my friend, who urged me to try to keep close to him. The road was crowded with a long line of horse-drawn wagons overloaded with goods and materials from the cooperative enterprises, stores and warehouses, with some people on top heading out of town eastwards, not knowing their destination or what awaited them. We continued our journey walking on the side of the road alongside the moving column of horse-drawn wagons, among those who accompanied the wagons and others, who, like us, had decided to leave. At noontime, we had a "bite" to eat while walking; a man who knew our family approached us and started to persuade us to return back home while we were not too far away from it. His argument was that we were young, by ourselves, with no means of survival to undertake such a risk. As for them, they were grown ups, ready to overcome unforeseen difficulties and hardship. His words hammered me over the head but I still did not follow his advice, an inside feeling told me not to do it and we continued walking with more vigor. One hour later another young man I knew ran up to us with a statement that literally flew out of his mouth "I've been looking for you all morning, trying to find you. Your Mother stopped me while I was leaving, she was crying and begged me to catch up with you and tell you to return home and, if you don't agree, you should send back your younger brother Meyer." His voice was so convincing that I could not withstand it. I pictured my mother's crying and suffering face. I could not take it. I asked him to return. Not saying a word, he obediently with the bag of food over his shoulder and left. I noticed tears in his eyes but he kept on going, disappearing in the crowd. I was heartbroken but kept on walking at a slower pace, thinking, was it right or wrong, what I just did. It was too late anyway and, most probably, this was our destiny. In the meantime, while my walking pace slowed down, our town wagons moved ahead and my friend with them. I could not find or catch-up with him, and have never seen him since.

I continued my journey now with people I didn't know. About an hour later I ran across two young men, one of them the brother of my sister-in-law, the other a neighbor of mine. They had decided to return, and urged me to go with them back home. They told me that the moving columns ahead of us had been air-raided and fired upon with machine guns and that there were a lot of casualties. This time I gave in and joined them. We walked backwards for about an hour, I was exhausted and hungry. We noticed a horse-drawn wagon approaching us. It was carrying some small printing machines and other equipment from the town's printing house. They stopped, so did we. We recognized the carrier, a young male employee, and with him a girl student from our high school, her name was Marilyn, we all knew each other. The moment she found out about our decision to go back, she yelled at us: "you are committing suicide," and calling us names, she suggested joining them on the wagon and going with them. I was thinking about it for a while and finally came to realize that she was right, probably sent by God to save my life. I got on the wagon, the other two refused and proceeded back home; we went forward

It was getting dark. We were passing a little hamlet, the carrier decided to give the horse a little rest and food, we needed it too. We stopped on the side of the road on a hay field, picked out the closest haystack and sat there. I was so exhausted that I didn't know even how and when I fell asleep. I opened my eyes, when I felt somebody pushing my shoulder, waking me. It was Marilyn, giving me bad news, by telling me that the carrier with the wagon disappeared. She was also sleeping and didn't hear anything, when he left or where. It was dawning. The sky was clear and blue, the field was wet from the early-dew, so were we. She had some clothing and food left on the wagon, but since it was gone, nothing else was left for us to do, than join the emerging movement on the road; we did so and continued our journey. The sun rose, it became warm, we were both tired and hungry. We noticed a rapidly approaching wagon with young men and women. We caught up with them asking to let us join them. They slowed down, someone extended a hand to Marilyn, I helped her and she was on the wagon. When I started to climb up, they pushed me down, saying there is no more room for me. I grabbed the wagon's back enclosure, trying to get on forcefully, but I was hit on my hands and pushed down. I was hurt. The wagon could not accommodate one more small skinny guy like me. But that is the way it was.

I proceeded on my journey following others, not knowing where I was going. One thing I knew for sure, that I have to aim my direction for a railroad station. I was also aware of the fact, that they were bombed, but since we were heading southeast, we were less exposed to them since the initial Nazi offensive attack took place in the center of the Ukraine. I was walking all day passing some cross-roads. Some people changed directions; I didn't, since I wasn't sure which one is the right one. When I asked my sojourners, they also had no idea, so I followed my instinct.

In the late afternoon, I entered a little town on the Soviet side already. I stopped by a little house; children were playing outside in the yard. I was thirsty, so I asked one of the kids for a drink of water. The mistress of the house appeared, she glanced at me, and right away she realized who I am. She invited me inside of the house, gave me some water, and sent me to wash up. I freshened up and told her my story. She was crying listening to me. Her husband arrived from work. It was a Jewish family, like a lot of others who could not make up their minds what to do. I had dinner with them, my first since I left. They offered me the chance to stay with them until the front would move away, and then I would be able to return home. They were very cordial and pleasant people who could not imagine or believe that anything wrong is going to happen. I politely declined their offer, and advised them to leave, telling them about rumors I had heard about Nazi atrocities which were at that time in the early stages. I stayed there overnight. In the morning, after having breakfast with them I expressed my thanks and appreciation for their cordiality, having me overnight, and feeding me, reminding them again of my advice to leave. Before I left, the lady of the house, crying, handed over a bag, in which later on I found a loaf of bread and a few wrapped sandwiches. I was again on the road, well rested with renewed strength heading east with a decreased number of wagons and people. In the afternoon, a horse-drawn wagon fully loaded with boxes and bags, and four men on top, was passing by. Two spare horses tied up to the back, followed the wagon. One of the carriers noticed me, asking whether I am willing to drive on the horses. I never was even close to a horse and was afraid of them, but I made the "courageous" decision and agreed, thinking that it's better riding than walking. They stopped. One of the men helped me to climb on the horse, gave me a little stick, and here I was horseback riding, turning instantly into a horseman. It was not as easy to ride a horse as I thought, especially without a saddle and with no experience. Using common sense I pressed my legs strenuously to the horse's body and held my hands by the neck, trying to keep my balance, and at the same time I also managed to hurry the horse, by hitting him slightly from time to time to keep in pace with the increased speed of the wagon. Little by little, I got used to the riding. We covered a good distance of mileage during the day. At nightfall we entered a village and stopped there. All four men went to a nearby house and ordered me to guard the wagon. I sat in the back corner of the wagon, had one of my sandwiches, and was waiting patiently. About one hour later they returned. Satisfied after a hot meal, they decided to rest. They all fell asleep in their sitting spots, so did I. Some funny noises awakened me. I opened my eyes and saw the men opening boxes, removing the contents and placing them in their own bags. I did not move and closed my eyes making believe that I don't see or hear anything. A little bit later came a command to wake up. The minute I tried to get off the wagon, I felt a pain in my rear end, which became blistery. I realized that I could not ride the horse anymore; I let them know what happened to me. Their answer did not surprise me, it was short and clear: there was no room for me on the wagon. Again on my own, I walked out slowly from the village. It was dawning, the road still empty, but becoming busy by sunrise with wagons and pedestrians, this time not only civilians but military men unarmed, with belts. According to their stories, they lost their units and were heading to the city of Vinnitza where new units are being formed. I also found out that the city is not too far away, a day or two walking distance. During the day, low-flying German aircraft flew by, but did not touch us. Late in the evening we entered a small town. We passed by a school building, stopped there and stayed overnight. During the night you could hear far away explosions which aroused fear and made us aware that the fighting continued. I also found out that the city of Vinnitza was just another eight - ten kilometers away, and that it is a big railway junction. At sunrise I was back on the move. This time I noticed road signs pointing in the direction of the city. I couldn't keep pace with the others because of the pain in my back. I was lagging behind but kept walking entering the city of Vinnitza before noon time. The streets were almost empty; I entered one big office building. Almost all the doors to the rooms were open, file and desk drawers open, books and a variety of documents, papers in disarray on top, and not a living soul present. It became clear to me that all State establishments had been evacuated. I got out, asked the first passer-by directions to the railroad station. I was told that the freight station was about one kilometer away and also given directions to get there. In about thirty minutes I reached the tracks not far away from the freight station. I must say that I was very lucky because suddenly I heard and noticed an arriving freight train approaching and slowing down in a very smooth motion, the car doors wide open, with railing barriers, not fully occupied with evacuees. A quick thought flashed through my mind, to catch up to the car while it moved slowly and climb in. In a matter of a few seconds I was running alongside the slow-moving car, grabbed the edge of the car floor, threw in my bag and with all the effort I could exert, I managed to climb into the car. My walking journey luckily came to an end.

On The Freight Train

No one from among those present, seeing a lonely, small skinny teen-ager, escaping from the Nazis, just like all of them were doing, desperately *trying* to climb in while the train was moving, extended a hand of help. On the contrary, instead of compassion, I heard voices of displeasure, saying that there was not enough room in the car for more people. In reality, the car was half empty, and the irony of fate was that we all ran to save our lives, nevertheless, selfishness and disregard was rooted in some people even in such horrible times. Not paying attention to the unfriendly remarks, I found a spot on the floor not far from the door. In the meantime, the train increased its speed, did not stop at the station, just as I suspected, my quick decision was correct. While I was resting and look-ing around, I noticed not only civilians but military men were present in the car also. I had some leftovers from my bag and napped for a while. When I woke up the train was at a standstill. I looked around trying to find a spot away from the door, when I noticed two familiar faces in the corner end of the car.

I didn't believe my eyes; I looked again and recognized two young men from our town a little bit older in age than me. When I approached them, they were pleasantly surprised, invited me to join them, and made a spot for me. I was very happy. I was not alone anymore. We heard the whistle of our locomotive; the train started moving, picking up speed. I found out from my new friends that the train was heading for Kazakhstan, a Soviet Republic in central Asia. At nightfall, we stopped again and did not move till the next morning. Since the train was at a standstill and we had no more food, I decided to get off the train, to look around and see whether I could find some food. It was early in the morning; our train was in the middle of a wheat field. Not far away a few little houses could be seen. I walked over to the front of the train and asked the supervisor whether he had some food for distribution–the answer was negative. As for how long we would stay there, he wasn't sure. Not far away I noticed a country track leading towards one of the houses visible on an elevated side. When I approached the house I noticed a sizeable village beyond it. That house happened to be a village store with a little bit of everything, divided in two parts, one half with groceries, the other half with fully loaded shelves of bread and other baked goods. A salesman or store manager was behind the counter. I asked him to sell me two breads, recalling meanwhile that I had no money. He solved my problem, stating that he was awaiting an arriving military unit for which the bread is designated and that's why he can't sell it. I walked out helplessly.

In the meantime, some other people from the train arrived, they also wanted to buy bread, and he refused. A scuffle started, people jumped over the counter grabbing loaves of bread and running away to the train. For a short while, I was undecided and afraid to act, but then I did just the same, and went back to the train with two loaves of bread under my arms. Shortly we got the green light and left. While I was away, my sojourners, found out that we were approaching the city of Odessa, and that our train would stop only at the freight yard. So they decided to get off there, assuming that the Germans will be stopped and pushed back eventually, thus, we would be better off remaining in a big city with good supplies. As for me, it was optional, to stay with them or to continue to central Asia. I decided to stay with them. I didn't want to be by myself again. Of course, their thinking was naive, because what we didn't know then is that the Red Army was in disarray retreating with very minimal resistance or no resistance at all, with heavy losses in killed and wounded, and entire units taken prisoner. We did find out about it the minute we entered Odessa, to which we came by getting off the train and taking the tram to the city. The city had a centre for evacuees where we got some financial help and a place for a temporary stay in a private home. We were also told that the city also got the order for evacuation to the rear of the country, so the best thing that was left for us to do was to catch the very first train available heading eastwards and leave as soon as possible. We stayed there for a couple of days with a very pleasant Jewish family, waiting for a train. We urged them to leave also, but they could not make up their minds about what to do, for a variety of reasons, financial, family problems, etc. and most importantly it was just the beginning of the war and it was unbelievable even to think that the turn of events would be so cruel, inhuman, tragic, and eventually would cost them their lives. Two days later we caught a freight train heading eastwards. Three days later we stopped in the city of Krasnodar.

Work on the Farms

City authorities sent us to the farming regions of the area to work in collective farms to help gather in the harvest. We worked there until the beginning of fall. In October, the three of us were transferred to a grain growing State farm in the Primorska-Achtarskiy region, close to the Sea of Azov, to take tractor driving courses. We were settled in a hostel located on a farmstead of that grain growing farm. It was a small settlement with a large repair work-shop, dining hall and general store. We received overalls for work and a modest allowance for self-support which was not bad during war time. In the beginning of winter, we worked five days per week in the workshop as helpers with assigned mechanics repairing and overhauling wheeled and caterpillar tractors, watching and learning while taking apart engines, replacing worn out parts with new ones, and assembling them. On the sixth day we studied the theory of internal combustion engines, transmissions, steering gear, etc. Everything was working out ok except for the bad news from the front. In the middle of the winter the Nazis captured the city of Rostov-on-Don but the Red Army repulsed them and took it over again. Our farm received orders to provide manpower to the front of that region to dig trenches. We were among them, but in separate teams. We left by train and arrived on a railroad junction, from where trucks picked us up to an outskirt of town where we had to dig. We were quartered in houses of the local population. The next morning each one received a loaf of bread; picks, spades and crow bars were handed out, and we went to work.

It was very cold and frosty, the ground frozen, our clothing definitely was not for a severe winter, but it was war time and the only thing that was left to do was to work hard in order not to become numb. As for a hot meal, we were at the mercy of the people we stayed with. During the night one could hear air craft roaring, mortar and machine gun fire, not far away. In the morning when we assembled to go to work, we found hand written leaflets encouraging us: "Do not worry. The German army will soon liberate you from the Jewish domination and the communist regime" and other trash. When we arrived at the trenches we noticed a group of workers standing in a circle and shouting loudly: "Who killed Christ? The Jews! Who invented and imposed Communism on us? The Jews! Who exploits us? The Jews!" etc. One of my fellow farm employees, a gypsy, pulled me aside and advised me to leave this place with him and return to the farm because he "smelled something no good and dangerous." We had no supervision from the farm, so not asking questions we took a long walk directly to the railroad station, caught an oncoming freight train back to the farmstead hostel, nobody asked us any questions. Very shortly my two fellow townsmen returned also. We stayed there until the early spring sowing campaign. In the beginning we were assigned to experienced tractor drivers as helpers. Later on I started to work on my own, on a wheeled tractor, ploughing, harrowing and sowing with a seeding machine with a helper on it. In July, when the harvesting campaign started I was transporting grains from the harvester to the threshing floor, and from there to the elevator. It happened to be a year of very good crop capacity, but unfortunately the Nazis kept advancing. It was just a little bit over a year since the war started, and a large part of the western U.S.S.R. was lost and occupied by the Nazis; on the north the Baltic republics, the city of Leningrad was almost encircled, they were on distant approaches to Moscow, White Russia and the Ukraine were taken, and the Nazis kept advancing to Stalingrad and to the south toward the Caucasian mountains, to the sources of oil. Our farm received orders to prepare for evacuation. Some farm reservists were called up for service, among them my two friends; only experienced tractor drivers were released because the farm needed them. As for me, at that time my age wasn't yet subject to the call up, so I remained on the farm helping to prepare the evacuation.

On the Road Again

One week later most of the tractor drivers from all branches spared from the call-up and some other farm employees, assembled on the farmstead with all the tractors, wheeled and caterpillar, with two or three hooked on wagons, loaded with bags with millet, sunflower seeds, dry fruits, barrels with salted pork, lard, salted poultry, honey and other produce and items that should not be left.

The rear of the column formation was locked up with a mobile kitchen tractor which pulled gasoline tanks, and grease barrels. We moved out before noon heading in the south-east direction towards the Caucasian mountains. I was driving a wheeled tractor with two wagons of wheat hooked on in the middle of the column. Until the afternoon, my driving was nice and smooth. Suddenly my steering wheel turned to the right and I could not straighten it out. I had to stop otherwise I would be on the side of the road. By exerting all my strength I managed to straighten it out, continuing to drive, holding the steering wheel strongly, but not for long. Once again I turned to the right. This time I could not straighten it out, my tractor was on the side of the road, stalled, with the wagons left on the road even before I managed to stop. The column kept on moving. One driver stopped and tried to help me. He checked out the situation, stating that the steering problem could not be repaired in the field, looked at me helplessly and left. I sat on the side of the road, scared, and thinking, was it an accident or foul play? Whatever it was, I couldn't leave it just like that. So I decided to wait for a while. In the meantime, the column disappeared, so did the roar of the tractors. It was quiet all around except for the noise of the birds circling above over my head and landing from time to time to feed themselves. I don't know how long I was sitting there waiting, it seemed like a lifetime to me. But I also felt that somebody from the remaining evacuees will pass by and pick me up. My hopes and feelings came true, when finally I noticed a jeep approaching and slowing down. It stopped and I recognized our farmstead jeep with our chief engineer driving, our director sitting next to him, and our agriculturist in the back seat. I walked over quickly and told them what happened. The chief engineer, not thinking too long, told me to get into the jeep, and we left. A few hours later we caught up with the column. We stopped next to a caterpillar tractor. The chief engineer ordered the driver to take me as a helper, and left. We continued to move ahead south-eastward on the plains of the Krasnodar and Stravapol territories for a few days. The roads became more crowded with evacuees from regional towns, collective and State farms, because all the traffic had to cross the one existing bridge in that particular area of the Kuban river. A very big crowd of people, trucks, tractors and horse-driven wagons accumulated on the road and the side of it, organizing turns for the long lines waiting to cross the bridge. We were very luck not to be air-raided by the Nazis who kept on advancing but didn't reach that particular area. At last, our turn came and we crossed the bridge. Very soon the plains ended and we noticed it in the change of the pictorial view of the country-side, we entered the area where the northern part of the Caucasian mountains begins. We stopped in a mountainous village, Ubinskaya, parked all tractors with the wagons of goods in a wooded canyon with a streamlet. All men were inducted in the Field Forces. Only the supply manager of the farm, an older man, the farm accountant, and wounded and discharged marine, Andrey, and myself, not old enough to be inducted, remained with all the equipment and supplies on our own. We found a temporary place of residence, in one of the houses in the village. In the meantime, retreating infantry units also moved into the village and took up positions on its outskirts. The Germans stopped in the neighboring village in front of us and entrenched themselves also. We found ourselves on the front line. The mountainous wooded area, with no roads or communication, with the temporarily retreating but still defending army units, and partisan detachments, were too frightening for the Germans to enter the village, so these and other reasons stopped them from advancing. But they kept on menacing us with daily bombing of the village with a -single frame-like plane. I was caught once in such an air raid with the son of the lady we stayed with, when we went to get some food stuffs form our parked wagons. Her house was on a hillside. As soon as we came down to the village road, we could hear the familiar roar of the infamous frame-like plane approaching. It was too late to return home, where we had a shelter so we looked around for some cover, and noticed a big chestnut tree with wide spread branches in the middle of the road, under it a young man calling us to hide under it also. I instantly refused realizing that it's too open and dangerous and pulled down the boy to the trench-like side of the road and lied down still. A minute later we heard the terrifying deafening noise of falling bombs and four consecutive explosions. It was very scary, especially the falling squeals of the bombs while you are lying down. At that moment I was thinking that at any second the bomb will penetrate my back and that will be the end. Thank God, it did not happen, we were very lucky. A few minutes later the roar of the plane became weaker and weaker, we realized that it had turned around and disappeared. We got up, walked over to the tree, and found the man that remained under it, lying on the ground, dead. It was a terrible and distressful picture, his face in a blood bath, cut off from his head, apparently with a fragment of one of the exploded bombs. We could not be of help in a situation like this. Luckily a military patrol showed up. They sent us away, telling us to go back home to the shelter. By that time the village became more and more crowded with retreating infantry, partisans and civilians. It also became a military formation point for the area. Two officers were also stationed with us in our temporary quarters. One evening they showed up with another man, vodka and snacks, and had some drinks. Our room was adjacently separated from theirs by a thin wall and door. We could hear a heated conversation about Jews. We went to sleep not paying attention to it, but were woken up by their loud drunken voices, especially of one man who was bragging how he was killing Jews, during their retreat from the city of Kerch, on the Crimean peninsula. I couldn't fall asleep after what I'd heard. I also noticed that Andrey was awake. The only one snoring was our supply manager. The next morning we decided to leave this place before the Germans enter it. There was no reason for us to remain there, not only because it became crowded, but it was late fall, damp and cold, plus the winter was approaching. Our plan was not an easy one, but there was no other choice. We had to cross the top of the Pshadskiy pass in order the reach the only railroad alongside the eastern part of the Black Sea leading to Tbilisi, the capital of Soviet Georgia. We notified our supply manager that we are leaving. He wasn't at all surprised at our decision, as for himself, he decided to stay. On the same day, we packed up two kit-bags with food and some clothing we had, and left.

Crossing the Mountain Pass

Neither of us knew directions to our planned destination but we started out our continuous journey firmly, *this* time again on foot, up to the mountains in a cloudy, damp fall morning. We were not surprised when we met a numerous body of people, civilians as well as military, already on the mountain paths also leaving the area. We kept on going up and up slowly, resting and having snacks on glades with leftover camp-fires by others; sometimes we had to start a camp-fire by ourselves when we were wet and cold, we had plenty of brushwood for that. During that mountain journey we also encountered deliveries of ammunition in boxes, loaded on donkeys and sizeable wooden boards dragged by horses on the ground. I don't remember exactly how long it took us to cross the pass, but I do remember two nights staying over on glades next to a camp-fire, turning from one side to another to warm up. Finally we started to go down. It was much easier and faster. Shortly after that we entered a small seaport with a radio station, Tuapse, located on the shore of the north-eastern part of the Black Sea. From there we caught the first on-coming freight-train heading toward Tbilisi on the only one existing railway on the sea-shore of the area. We had two stopovers, one in the city of Sachi and the other in the city of Sukhumi before we reached our destination., Tbilisi, in the late evening, where we stayed overnight in the railway station.

Tbilisi

The station was very busy and crowded with traveling military personnel as well as civilians. The waiting rooms were so packed, that not only couldn't we find a place to sit, but to stand. We made our way somehow to a free corner on the floor and accommodated ourselves. We had a snack and fell asleep.

We were woken up by a cleaning man early in the morning. Many of the people had left, the place was half-empty. We went outside to freshen up and look around, but not for long; it was late in October, raining and cold, so we returned took a seat on a bench and discussed our next move.

Andrey planned to go back home to Vologda, a city located about 450 miles East of Leningrad. He invited me to go with him but I couldn't. I had no documents. It was easier for him, he was a discharged, wounded marine; he was entitled and had free food provision and transportation. As for me, from the moment we left the front line village, I was in effect a displaced person. No documents were required while on the farm, which I was no longer associated with. To undertake once more, such a long, complicated, roundabout journey from the South to the North to get to his hometown, without money, winter clothes and weak and exhausted, was too much for me. Besides, at that time, most of the western part of Russia was occupied by the Nazis and embraced in fierce battles: Leningrad was surrounded and blockaded. I politely declined his invitation and shared my plans with him, which were to remain in Tbilisi if possible, try to seek help from the City Authorities to find a job or training and get settled here until the war was over. We chatted for a while; I expressed my thanks and appreciation for his generosity. We shook hands wishing each other good luck and he left. I have not seen or heard from him since.

Again by myself in the railroad station, I started to think about my next step for survival. I found myself in a difficult situation because I had reached the age of sixteen and was now required to have a passport, but having no residence I did not qualify; without it, I could not get registered in the City, apply for work or make any other move for that matter. Unfortunately, the station did not have a Centre for evacuees, the first source for immediate responsive help in my situation. Since I was a complete stranger to the City, with no money, I could not go right away to search for it, besides I didn't speak Georgian, Russian was not popular and the local people did not respond willingly to it.

So, I decided to stay for a while in the station which provided me with a temporary roof over my head, and the possibility to try to earn some money by carrying luggage for arriving passengers, till I would be able to contact responsible authorities and ask for help. I mingled with the crowd all day, looking for somebody older, with more life experience, for advice. Two persons took interest in listening to the story of my situation; one advised me to look outside for drunkards, pull them aside, and take their valuables and leave, a thing I would never do. The other one made clear to me, that I could not get residency and be registered in the City, but should try hard to find a way out of my situation and stay alive, because those who will remain alive after the war is over, will have a prosperous life. Late in the evening, I found a spot in a corner of the floor, had some leftover food and fell asleep with my kit -bag under my head. I was woken up by the loudspeakers announcement to leave the premises for cleaning. I got up, and only then I noticed that my kit bag with some remaining clothes still from home was gone. I was upset for a while but calmed down and didn't take it to heart. It was daybreak. The advice of the second person became so imprinted in my memory that always when I had to overcome difficulties, I could hear his encouraging words in my ears, and it was helpful.

I went outside to the front of the station exits to meet and find passengers wanting luggage carriers. After a while, they started to disembark from the arriving trains. but most of them with light luggage ran to the nearby trams, buses or taxis; no luck for me this time. It was a cloudy, cool and grey October day.

I had to wait for the next train which was a suburban, with local farmers delivering fruits, vegetables and dairy products to the market. One farmer accepted my offer of help. He tied up two bags, one with apples, the other with dry fruits and threw it over my shoulder, then gave me a small bag with walnuts and we left. It took us twenty to twenty-five minutes to reach the market. He gave me some money, an apple and some dry fruits. I was very happy. These were my first earnings since I left the farm

I spent some time walking around the market, where to my surprise I could see a large variety of all types of goods and other goods in abundance, no rationing, the only thing one needed was money. I had no problem getting back to the station. A few block before it I noticed a man carrying a suitcase in one hand and a metal container in the other. I caught up with him, offered my help. He stopped, looked at me, agreed, and then handed me the container telling me to follow him. We kept walking for a long time. I was trying to remember the street names and other points of orientation to find my way back. While we were walking a smell of gasoline hit my nose, I also felt that my pants on the right side of my legs became wet. It occurred to me that the container had a leak coming from the cap, I tried to tighten it. I couldn't. Luckily we reached our destination; I got paid and went back to the station stopping by at the market place to buy some food. I returned to the station in the late afternoon exhausted. The place was not so crowded this time. I found a spot on the bench, had some food and napped for a while. I was woken up shortly by a station guard who was checking train tickets. I had to leave, since only transit passengers could stay overnight in the station. I went outside. It was dark and cold. I had to find a place to stay over-night. I tried again to sneak in, but was chased out this time also. While walking near the Station, I approached the platform fence. My attention was caught by a group of young men climbing over it and running to a standing train on the tracks, entering it through the passage door at the end of the car. It dawned on me that this is the place where I should try to stay overnight. Not giving it a second thought I followed in their footsteps and did the same thing. While in the car I found out from one of the young men that this is a long-distance train. Its destination is Yerevan, capital of Armenia; it arrives there in the morning and returns to Tbilisi in the evening. He also advised me to watch out for the train conductor, if I don't want to get kicked off the train, especially after stopover rounds. I climbed up to an upper berth, usually designated for luggage in the middle of the car and laid down, In the meantime, boarding started. I could hear the conductor's voice asking passengers to present tickets. This was a third class carriage with open compartments, no assigned seats , on a first-come, first-serve basis. Shortly, the train started off, slowly picking up speed. I became drowsy but was afraid to fall asleep so I tried to overcome it by climbing down, walking out to the platform and freshen up with fresh air for a while, then I returned to my spot. We made several stops. Some passengers got off and some boarded. Suddenly I heard a stern voice asking to produce tickets. I quickly climbed down and went to the platform on the opposite side from where the voice was coming. The train was running at full speed. I opened the door carefully, took two steps down, holding on firmly to the handrails, hoping to evade the conductor's sight, then I closed the door and waited for him to cross over to the other carriage.

A short while later I went cautiously back to my place, lied down and fell asleep momentarily. Luckily, nobody bothered me anymore until the train reached its destination, Yerevan. I got off and went into the station. It was a nice, clear morning but I decided to stay inside, have a snack and rest for a while, During the entire day I was in and out of the station, looking around trying to find passengers who needed help to carry their luggage, but in vain, So, disappointed, I decided to return to Tbilisi, which I was already a little bit used to. The same evening, I sneaked in almost in the same way I did the night before in Tbilisi. Using the same tricks not to get caught by the conductors, I arrived back with no incidents. When I got off the train this time, I felt like I was back home. Everything looked old and familiar to me in spite of the fact that I had been there for just several days. While in the station, I had a snack, rested for a while and then I went outside to try to earn some money. I have to admit that this time I was more fortunate than days before. I carried stuff to and from the market till late afternoon, earning more money than I expected. On the way back from the market I bought myself a good lunch. Luckily, I had no problem getting in to the station this time. I found a spot on a bench next to a group of accommodated travelling military personnel and had my late lunch.

My Arrest

While sitting quite full, but exhausted from a full day's work, I realized that I had to stop this way of life; wandering, sleeping on trains or stations with no place to live; it was a manner of living which eventually would turn me into a vagrant. Of course all of this arose from the situation I was in, but I could not let it go on. My thoughts brought me back to my earlier decision, to apply for a passport without which I could not make any move whatsoever. Now since I made some money, I could use it for buses or trams to get me to the passport division of the City Militia or to other city authority offices to ask for help. I decided firmly to find out the addresses and locations of these offices the first thing in the morning. Occupied with these thoughts I did not notice that it's getting late. I was tired, drowsy, and feel asleep while sitting. The turns of the following events, which occurred after midnight, helped me to accomplish my plans in an unpleasant but much easier way than I had intended.

While sleeping on the bench I had a dream that I was running away from the conductor who was following me, grabbing and pulling me while I tried to free myself, but couldn't. I opened my eyes but did not see or understand what was going on at first Normally, I sleep very soundly, but this time I was knocked out completely after carrying a lot of loads almost all day. Finally, I woke up and noticed two Militia men in front of me, one of them shaking my shoulder. I sobered up and realized that this could be trouble or my wandering had come to an end. I was asked to produce my documents and ticket, neither of which I had. All of my efforts to explain my situation didn't work. I was arrested and escorted to the regional Militia Station.

They put me in a cell with several other men. The cell had a bare concrete floor with plank beds hinged and locked to the wall during day time. One hour later, I was called for finger printing and then escorted back to the cell, where I was met with joking questions about how my "piano lesson" went. I answered in the same manner and went back to sleep. We were woken up by the noise of a bell at rising time, which was six o'clock in the morning. When I got up I felt a burning and itching on the right side of my leg. I checked it out and noticed a rash over it. I decided to notify the very first official I saw about it. At seven-thirty everyone got a bowl of soup with a slice of bread.

One hour later, I was called out, escorted to an interrogator. He started out with a barrage of questions: who am I, why no documents, no train tickets and finally why was I sleeping on the train. I gave him briefly the story of my situation, noticing a sarcastic smile on his face when I mentioned the two words "tractor driver." I concluded my story with a plea for help to settle down here and put an end to my homelessness for which I would need a passport to begin with.

He did not answer for a while. Glancing at me and then looking at his desk, he continued coolly: "We do not register evacuees, or any other newcomers for that matter, in this city, but because of your situation I will refer you to the passport division with instructions to help you." He wrote a note, sealed it in an envelope with the address on it, handed it over to me saying "The place is not too far away, must a few blocks." Explaining how to get there, he wished me good luck and released me.

I got there very quickly. A guard stopped me at the entrance: "Why are you here, and who do you want to see, he asked me. Instead of answering I handed over the addressed envelope. He looked at it, then telling me to wait; he went to a nearby telephone and made a phone call. Shortly an escort showed up and asked me to follow him. He led me into one of the offices located in a long corridor and told me to wait. He left and I sat down waiting A few moments later, a side door opened and a middle-aged lady dressed in civilian clothing with a pleasant appearance entered the room with a folder in her hand. She sat down at her desk, looked at me with an appraising expression on her face, read the note she received from the interrogator, then turned to me asking, "Tell me your story." I did. She listened carefully with a softening compassionate face. When I finished, she replied softly, "We will help you." She took a deep breathe and continued. "At first we will direct you to a doctor to ascertain your age, and then we will issue you a temporary passport and try to arrange something for you. When she mentioned the word doctor, I recalled the rash on my leg and told her about it. She responded very swiftly, giving me a referral to a dermatological clinic and directions to get there. She also told me to come back with the results, to see her after my discharge from the clinic.

The Clinic

Satisfied with the way things were developing, I was heading towards the clinic with new hope that my wandering was coming to an end. I took the tram and arrived at the clinic at noon time.

The receptionist checked my referral note and told me to wait until called. A little bit later I was called into the doctor's office. A young Georgian physician met me at his desk. He asked me to have a seat on the examination bed and give him a little background about myself. Briefly, I told him about my situation. He listened carefully, and then examined my leg asking "Did you spill some fuel on it?" I did not answer right away. I don't know why but I blanked out completely for a moment and forgot completely about the leaking gasoline container I carried for somebody a few days before, but it came back to me and I recalled what happened, telling him, "That's the case." He took another good look at both sides of my leg, washed his hands, returned to his seat and told me: "We will admit you to the clinic and let you stay overnight I will consult in the morning with another dermatologist and establish whether or not it is a burn, rash or an infectious disease."

He ordered the nurse to take me to one of the rooms on the skin ward. She escorted me to a four patient bedroom, gave me a tagged bag with my name on it for my clothes, handed over bed clothes and robe and ordered me to take a shower. Then pointing to an unoccupied bed, she left.

Not giving it much thought, I went to a little dressing area next to the shower, undressed, put my clothes in the bag provided and took a long overdue shower. Relieved and refreshed, I went to my designated bed in clean pajamas and lay down relaxing.

This was the first time since we were evacuated from the farm that I was resting in a clean bed. My thoughts took me back to the moment we started the long journey to the foot of the Caucasian mountains, visualizing all the things that happened to me. I recalled crossing the mountain pass, sleeping in the woods under a bare sky next to a campfire, with mostly cloudy and rainy weather. Then traveling in freight passenger trains and finally living in railroad stations. My thoughts were interrupted as meal time was approaching and food service personnel started to deliver dinner to the patients.

I had my meal, became drowsy and fell asleep. The next day, I was examined by two dermatologists on the morning rounds. They prescribed some ointment, told the nurse to apply it on my leg twice during day time and once before bed-time and left. I was discharged a day later with a statement that my rash is not infectious and will heal soon.

With a sense of relief, I reported back to the lady at the passport division who referred me to the clinic. I gave her my discharge statement; she read it with an expression of satisfaction. For a while she was sitting taciturnly and writing. She broke the silence saying. "This time I am referring you to a doctor who will ascertain your age. She gave me an addressed, sealed envelope and directions. I had no difficulty finding the doctor's office. He looked me over after I undressed and asked me: "when were you born?" August 28, 1926, I replied, giving him my date of birth, "Now you can put on your clothes and have a seat in the waiting room." I did just that. After a short while, the nurse gave me a certificate confirming the age ascertained by the doctor, to be handed over to the passport division, and I left.

The Trade School

With the certificate in my pocket, I reported back to the passport division. I gave the lady the certificate, she looked at it and directed me to take a picture in one of the rooms in the same building, and then to sit in the waiting room and wait until called

After a prolonged stretch of time I was called in to her office, she invited me to have a seat and made the following statement: "Since we can't register you in this city, and can't find employment for you in your situation, we are directing you to a trade school located in the small town of Manes, in the Alaverdi region, in one of our neighboring Union Republics, Armenia. Having said this she gave me my temporary passport, a sealed letter to the chairman of the district executive committee, who was also overseeing recruitment for that trade school, some money for a train ticket and other small expenses, and continued, " Since you have no place to stay, I would advise you to leave tonight." She wished me all the best and I left in a very good mood. I would have liked to know more about the school, but I realized that I would find out soon enough, so I didn't ask.

I caught the tram at a nearby stop and took it to the railroad station. On the way I returned to the street market where I used to spend the tips I earned carrying luggage. Since all official stores only accepted ration tickets, it was the only place I could buy food for cash.

It was dark when I arrived at the station. I went right away to the ticket hall and found out that my train is leaving late in the evening. So I had to wait about four more hours. I found a spot on the bench and since I hadn't eaten the whole day, my stomach reminded me that it was time to have a bite. Having relieved my hunger, I took a spot on the ticket line.

This time I boarded the train lawfully with a ticket in my hand. I climbed up to the middle berth, after asking the conductor to wake me up at my stop. A short while later the train started off, picking up speed. After such a busy day, running back and forth from one place to another, I fell asleep right away. Finally, the path ended on a plateau with a small settlement. It was early afternoon.

I could see students in uniforms entering a big structure which was a diner, as I found out later. Not too far away stood another building. The appearance of it made me feel that this was the administrative building, and I was right. I walked over and entered a small, modestly furnished waiting area with some offices located in a connecting corridor. I rested for a while, then notified the secretary that I was here to see the director, and gave her the letter addressed to him. I was called into his office,

I was received by a man in his late forties. He offered me a seat and asked me to tell him a little bit about myself He listened carefully as I related how I came to be in his office. When I concluded my story, he gave a deep sigh, saying, "We will accept you to our school gladly. I will assign you to a group that is being trained in prospecting drilling technique. The teaching is being conducted in Armenian, since the majority of the students are Armenian. However, the instructor also knows Russian, so there will be no language problem. He also has in his group, another Russian student. You will get to know each other and feel better." He picked up the phone and made a call. Then he turned to me saying, "I just spoke to the boarding manager, she will arrange everything for you and set you up in the same dormitory room with the Russian student, so you will not feel isolated.

Shortly, a lady showed up in his office, he introduced me to her as a new student, and asked her to take care of me. She asked me to follow her and we left. We didn't walk too far as we entered another structure which was the store house. She ordered one of her employees to issue me a complete uniform set and underwear to fit my size and to show me the way to the bath house. Then she turned to me saying, "After you take your bath, come back here and we will show you your quarters, It took us about fifteen minutes to get there.

I was lucky because the bath house was operating on that day. Usually, it was open twice a week only. I went inside of an almost empty, sizeable room with a concrete floor, a few drainage grills in the middle of the floor, a few shower heads and faucets on one side of the wall, concrete seats on the remaining walls, and a few wooden benches in the center. In one of the corners, a pile of tin wash basins with handles about fourteen or fifteen inches in diameter were stacked-up. Most of the twenty or thirty students that would use the bathhouse at one time had to use the basins to collect water from the faucets. It was a luxury to have my own bar of soap. After having a shower, putting my clothes in a marked bag and freshening up, dressed in a new uniform I went back to see the boarding manager. She was a Russian native, in her late thirties with a very pleasant appearance, and apparently good natured. "You see, she said meeting me at the entrance," you look like a new kopek. Asking me to follow her, she leads me to the dormitory. It was late afternoon. The students were back in their rooms from field training. We entered one of the rooms, with four beds, where I was assigned to stay.

Three students lodged in that room were present. One of them, Nikolay Belonogov, was the Russian student from the group I was assigned to. She introduced me to them, pointed out my bed and night table, saying "You can go with them to the dining hall for supper, everything was arranged." She wished me good luck and left. I had an introductory conversation with Nikolay, a teenager as I was, almost the same height, with a fair, freckled and kind face, telling him briefly about myself He did likewise. What I found out was that he also was an evacuee from Novorossiysk, a seaport on the northern side of the Black Sea. The next morning, after a restful night's sleep, I went with Kolya (that's how I called him from that moment on) for breakfast. The dining hall could accommodate over one hundred students at one time, ten students at a table. Four waitresses served breakfast which consisted three hundred grams of bread, a bowl of soup, tea and sugar.

The Training Period

After breakfast we went to one of the classrooms where I attended my first lesson. The instructor, who was notified about me ahead of time, welcomed me very warmly in Russian with a very heavy accent. He filled me in on what I had missed so far, briefly summarized. At one o'clock we had a two course dinner, soup and porridge with two hundred grams of bread. After dinner we went out for field training.

Not too far away from the settlement grounds, a structure with open sides and roof only was built. Within it, a drilling rig with a transmission belt to a motor and knife switch control was installed. There was also a water supply system. Before we started the drilling procedures we got instructed about safety precautions and how to conduct ourselves during the training. We spent about three hours drilling, removing the contents we got from the depths for analysis. After cleaning up the work area, we went back to school, washed up and went for supper, which had the same menu as breakfast except for the bread portion which was reduced from three hundred to two hundred grams. That was the main variety.

In the Hospital

And that's how my training began. It went routinely for about a week until one morning I woke up with a bad headache and fever. It was very hard for me to get up. Kolya helped me to get dressed and took me to the aid station. The nurse checked my temperature and got scared. It was very high. She notified my instructor, who showed up after a while. She told him that I have to be taken to a hospital immediately. I realized that much, but couldn't imagine how it could be done. It was a long way down a pathway, the students knew that well and had no desire to carry me. The instructor had to use all his persuasion skills to convince them that I was in real danger and they had no other means for transportation, so the only choice was to carry me. Finally, he got their cooperation. When the loud arguments ended, four students carried me out on a stretcher. They were followed by my instructor and, from the voices I faintly heard, at least two others for periodic relief.

Suddenly I was on the ground. I could hear the instructor trying to stop some of the boys from running away. Apparently he overcame their resistance because I was carried again. I don't know how long I was carried, but when I revived I was in the hospital bed, feverish and half unconscious. A nurse was sitting next to my bed bent over trying to feed me with biscuits and sweet tea, but I had no desire to any food, she had to force the teaspoons into my mouth, but it came back, I couldn't swallow it… Eventually, she succeeded in forcing some of it and left. I was very weak and didn't know what was happening around me. I also don't remember seeing a doctor. I fell asleep. When I woke up the lights were on, dim and weak, but blinding to my eyes. I got up, ran out into the corridor, running back and forth making noises, I was delirious. A nurse ran out from the nursing station, grabbed me and lead me back to my room, locked the door and left. I tried to open it, banged and shouted, not realizing what I was doing. There was no response anyway. Exhausted, I went back to bed and fell asleep.

The next morning I felt a little bit better. At breakfast time I was fed again by the same nurse. Only now I could see a very pleasant young lady with a kind face. I tried to feed myself but my hands were shaky, so she helped me. She was very nice to me; if not for her, who knows what would have happened to me.

Later in the morning, doctors' rounds started. I was examined by a doctor with a very stern look, not asking or saying anything. Then he checked the other two patients. One of them told him something pointing to me. I couldn't understand what he was saying; they spoke in a language I couldn't identify. I was left with an anxiety I couldn't overcome. The next day, he head nurse came into the room and gave me the "good" news that I was being discharged that day, not giving me any reason or explanation. It was a shock to me, I couldn't believe it. I asked her, "Can I see the doctor?" "No, he is not in today," was the answer and she left. I sat on the bed for a while stunned, thinking what can or should I do. I got my bag with the clothing from my locker, and slowly started to get dressed. While doing that I was thinking and trying to guess why I was discharged so early, still not well enough to take a few steps because of my weakness and dizziness, not to mention a three-mile walk up the hill to the school. It was a painful question that left me only with suspicions.

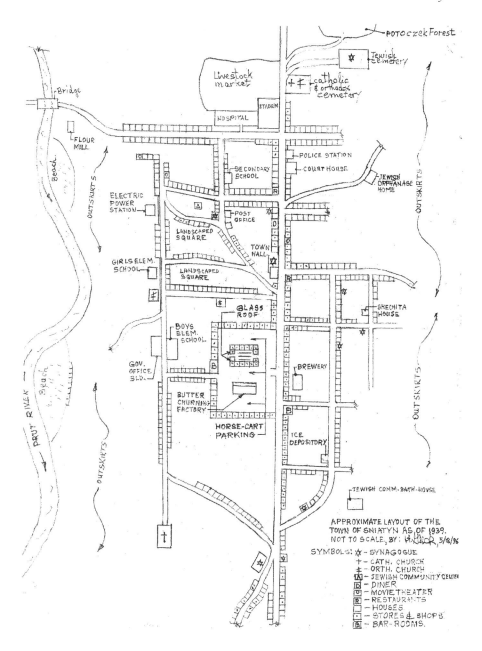

POTOczek Forest

✡ Jewish cemetery

Livestock market

✝ ✝ catholic & orthodox cemetery

STADIUM

Bridge

HOSPITAL

FLOUR MILL

POLICE STATION

COURT HOUSE

OUTSKIRTS

SECONDARY SCHOOL

JEWISH ORPHANAGE HOME

ELECTRIC POWER STATION

Ⓐ

POST OFFICE

OUTSKIRTS

LANDSCAPED SQUARE

TOWN HALL

GIRLS ELEM. SCHOOL

LANDSCAPED SQUARE

SHECHITA HOUSE

GLASS ROOF

BOYS ELEM. SCHOOL

BREWERY

GOV. OFFICE BLD.

Ⓑ

OUTSKIRTS

BUTTER CHURNING FACTORY

HORSE-CART PARKING

Ⓑ

ICE DEPOSITORY

PRUT RIVER

Beach

Beach

OUTSKIRTS

JEWISH COMM. BATH-HOUSE

APPROXIMATE LAYOUT OF THE TOWN OF SNIATYN AS OF 1939. NOT TO SCALE. BY: H. GLICK 5/8/96

SYMBOLS: ✡ – SYNAGOGUE
✝ – CATH. CHURCH
☦ – ORTH. CHURCH
Ⓐ – JEWISH COMMUNITY CENTER
Ⓓ – DINER
Ⓜ – MOVIE THEATER
Ⓡ – RESTAURANTS
☐ – HOUSES
☐ – STORES & SHOPS
Ⓑ – BAR-ROOMS.

Map of the town Sniatyn, Poland (1939) drawn from memory by Henry Glick

Glick Family Portrait
Henry is third from left. Morris, his one surviving brother, is standing first on
left, next to his Mother.
A tenth child was born to the family after this photo was taken.
The family surname was originally Glück but the "ü" was changed to the
Russian equivalent of "i" when Henry joined the Russian army.

Portrait of Henry's Father, Joseph Glück

Henry, early in his military service

Henry's sister

Henry's sister

Henry's sister, Hannah, dressed for the role of Esther in a play put on as part of the celebration of the Jewish holiday "Purim"

Henry as a soldier in the Russian Army

Wedding Portrait, Henry and Sonia Glick
(1951)

Family Portrait taken in Russia (1956)

Aboard the "Batory" headed for Montreal (1960)

Boris, Sonia, Joseph and Henry Glick
Family Portrait taken in Poland (1959)

Henry Glick, near the end of military service

Back to School

I was so upset when I left the hospital that I couldn't recall how I got to the pathway leading to the school. I do remember ascending it. It was a long, painful, drag. I reached the school grounds in the afternoon completely exhausted. The assistant director met me outside of his office. He noticed my condition and his first question was, "Why did they discharge you so early?" I made a helpless gesture with my hands, telling him briefly, "I don't know." That was all that I could tell him. Asking me to follow him, he led me to the dining hall. He ordered the manager to serve me dinner, and provide me with a double portion (of soup only) every day until further notice. He also told me that I was released for three days from field training. After dinner I went back to my room. Kolya was very glad to see me back. The next morning my instructor visited me, he wished me to get well and continue the training. I expressed my appreciation for his effort and help in taking me to the hospital. He was of Greek origin, very compassionate, and lived nearby in a small colony of Greeks about half a mile away, up in the hills. A small number of them were employed in the school. Very often, one could hear shouts of communication from above down to the school and vice-versa.

After three days of rest my condition improved significantly. I went back to the school routine attending classes and training. Apparently, the increased ration of soup helped me a little bit. But it also had its negative effect; it was thin and not too nourishing. As a result, I almost lost control of my bladder, especially while sleeping, so I stopped having my double portions.

It was springtime. We had sunny and cloudy days up there in the mountains. The temperature was mostly on the cool side. One Sunday, the only day off for the week, was exceptionally bright, sunny and warm. I invited Kolya to go outside for a stroll. He was not in the mood and refused, so I went by myself. Suddenly, while still not too far from the school grounds, I could hear some noises and laughter. I returned back, realizing that the noises were coming from the dormitory. I ran up the stairs to my room, opened the door, and if I hadn't seen what was going on, I wouldn't have believed it. Kolya was laying with his back on the floor, knocking with his fists and feet on the floor unconscious, surrounded by a group of laughing and noisy students. "What's going on?" was my question to all of them. There was no answer. Instead, one of the students slapped him across his face and he regained consciousness. I helped him to get up; he sat on his bed not saying a word. In the meantime, the students gradually disappeared.

We were sitting for a while silently. Then I broke the silence asking, "What did they do to you to put you in such a convulsive state?" "One of the students taught me that trick," was his reply. What I do, he continued, is I tie a towel around my neck and gently starts to squeeze it for a fraction of a minute, after which I loose consciousness and start to convulse. To regain it, somebody has to slap me across my face. I advised him not to let them use him for their entertainment by endangering his health. He accepted my advice, thanking me.

The next day, one of the students who took part in that ordeal stopped me on the balcony of the dormitory, insulted me using derogatory language, and pushed me, asking, "Why did you stop us from having fun?" "Because it was a humiliation of a friend of mine and not fun," I answered. I responded with a similar push and *told* him to stop pushing, echoing his abusive language. I had no desire to get engaged in a fight that he was trying to start. A cleaning lady who walked by stopped us by stepping in between us, only then he left, continuing to swear. I was glad it ended that way. The incident reached the office of the director, where I was portrayed as the instigator.

Assignment to Work

During the final days of our training, our instructor discussed with us the availability and possibilities of employment. Most of the available jobs were in the mines. He also informed us about possibilities of employment in the geological prospecting party to locate deposits of copper in a neighboring settlement, and recommended that we go there and inquire.

By the end of June our training had come to an end. Representatives from the copper mines of the area appeared in school for recruitment. During one of the meetings we had with the recruiters, I overheard a conversation between them and my instructor, conducted in Armenian. At the time when the only language I heard all the time was Armenian, I managed to master and learn the language sufficiently to catch most of the content of the conversation. The recruiter talked about manual loading of copper ore into small wagons on a narrow-gauge railway line, to be driven out of the mine and unloaded. My instructor pointed at me, telling the recruiter that I was a very hard working, obedient student and recommended me to be hired. I got a pitiful and sarcastic look, with disapproval on his face, when he compared me, a little, skinny, undernourished guy, with the native, well-fed and taller students.

The next day, before another general briefing, I asked my instructor to give me and my friend Nikolay permission to go and inquire about employment with the Geological Prospecting Party. He agreed with no hesitation and also gave us a written recommendation. Not wasting any time, we left right after the meeting on foot to the neighboring settlement where their personnel office was located. It took us about an hour and a half or two to get there because of the mountainous character of the area, with only pathways and no roads. The place we entered was a mining settlement with scattered, small native dwellings, houses, and apartment buildings and a variety of other structures. We had no problem finding the office building. It was an elongated, one-story building with a number of offices. We stopped at the receptionist's window, told her why we were there, and handed over our recommendation letter. After a ten minute wait, we were called into the office of the Chief Engineer. He asked us to give him a brief summary about ourselves, which we did. He listened to our stories very carefully, afterwards he told us to fill our application forms, leave them with the secretary, and come back in three days.

We went back to school with promising and encouraging expressions from our interview with the Chief. He was a tall, slim fair man in his late thirties or early forties, with a pleasant appearance and a constant, never disappearing smile on his face. On our way out I was stopped by his secretary, who managed to look over my application form, telling me that her origin is from the same place as I was from. She spoke to me a little in broken Polish, thus I had an acquaintance in the office of the Chief. Two days later Nikolay and I were called to our director's office. Our instructor was present also. He informed us that he received a call from the Chief of the Geological Prospecting Party, that we had been hired, and that we should go to Personnel as soon as possible to finalize the hiring process. Not wanting any more delays, we went again to the office of Personnel. We arrived there around lunchtime. The secretary introduced us to a team leader and told us to see her before we left. He gave us general information about the work. Our starting date would be the first of the week. He took us to the dormitory which was not too far away, introduced us to the overseer, telling her to provide us with bedding to show us the room in which we were going to stay. Turning to us he added that we can take residence whenever we are ready. We had lunch and went back to the office. The secretary gave us additional forms to be filled out and signed. She also gave us ration cards for bread for one month, seven hundred grams per day.

Satisfied and happy, we went back to the school. Our instructor met us, congratulated us, and led us to Supply, where we received new sets of uniforms. Nikolay got a full set. I didn't get a winter jacket, they didn't have my size. They told me to come back in a couple of weeks to get it.

On the Job

Early in the morning, a day before our starting date, we took our belongings and left for our new place and took up residence in the dormitory where we were assigned to stay. We reported our arrival to the overseer. She showed us the room and the beds we would occupy, then left. It was an ordinary place for singles, modestly furnished. Most of the occupants were conscripted laborers or veterans released from service for various reasons, who could not return to their place of origin because of the German occupation. After breakfast, we met with the team leader in his office, from where he took us to one of the drilling rigs. He introduced us to the crew as new apprentices, showed us around and told us to be observant and follow the sequence of all operations.

And that's how we started working; watching and learning. We worked only during the day shift, walking to and from work, there was no transportation available. We ate in a diner sponsored by the mining industry. The food was not bad, considering it was wartime. But for me, that work period was brief. In the middle of October I was called to the office of the chief engineer. The secretary handed me a letter from the regional military registration and enlistment office with instructions to appear before a military medical commission board immediately. She also told me to go and see the chief engineer. He received me with his usual smile, apologizing for not managing to arrange a request for a deferral, which he could have done, but he did not expect a call up so soon. He asked me to stop by with the screening results and then he will see what can be done. I expressed my thanks and on that note I left. Next day, early in the morning, I descended from the mining settlement to the regional township of Manes, and reported to the induction station. The place was crowded with draftees. The officer on duty registered me and told me to wait until called. I didn't wait too long. My name was called among three others. We undressed and entered the examination room. Three physicians, one woman and two men in white uniforms were sitting behind tables. The lady doctor examined my vision and gave me an okay, though the visibility in my left eye was almost zero. The other doctor looked me over and then ran two spread fingers from the neck down my front and back and gave me an ok also, telling me to wait for an assignment. While waiting, my attention was drawn to the crowd of draftees, all of them Russians. Here I am in Armenia, in one of the Caucasian Soviet Republics, and could not see any natives among the numerous waiting crowd. One hour later I was called to the office of the assigning officer. He handed me a sealed envelope with the following statement "We are sending you to a very good military unit stationed in the City of Leninakan. Before you leave this station, stop by at Supply Service, where you will receive a dry ration for three days and some money for transportation. Settle accounts with your company and report immediately to your assigned unit." On that note, I left and did exactly was I was told to do.

Nikolay was very upset when he found out that I was inducted for military service. He was accustomed and attached to me, he cried a little bit, but calmed down eventually. He and two other friends I got acquainted with during my brief stay in the dormitory, invited me to a farewell lunch. It so happened that they were my landsmen wounded in action and demobilized from active duty, with nowhere to go, the area they lived in was still occupied by the Germans. We enjoyed the lunch, then saying good-bye to each other, we parted. Three days later, I was on my way to my assigned unity, in the city of Leninakan.

In the Military Service

I arrived there at noon time. The first thing on my mind when I entered the railroad station was to look for a military patrol. I spotted one on duty outside in front of the station; a sergeant and soldier armed with submachine guns, walking slowly and observing the surrounding area. I approached them, inquired and got directions to my unit.

It took me about an hour and half to get there since the place was located on the outskirts of the other side of town. Finally, I noticed a fenced compound of barracks and buildings, training grounds, and a guard standing next to a booth near the entrance gates. I approached him and handed him the envelope. He glanced at it, went inside the booth and made a telephone call. Shortly, a soldier on duty showed up telling me to follow him to the staff headquarters.

I was met by a senior lieutenant who took my envelope and told me to wait. After a while he called me in to his office telling me: "Your documents are complete and in order. I am assigning you to the first company of our field engineer battalion. Now you will go and report to the master sergeant of the company and he will take care of the rest."

Escorted by a soldier on duty we left to the assigned company. We stopped near a long, one story barrack which I entered. My escort left. I told the soldier on duty that I am here to report to the master sergeant. He led me to his office, which was located in the corner of the barrack entrance. I didn't have to say a word, when I entered his office, he welcomed me, knowing that I am a new recruit, telling me to sit down, he scrutinized me. I also had a chance to observe him. He was a heavy set, taller than average man with a strict appearance on the first glance. After a brief silence he began to speak: "You are joining a newly formed company of young recruits. From now on you are one of us, and this will be your home. I will arrange your provisions, issue you a complete set of military uniform, and appoint a soldier who will escort you to the bath-house, so you can bring back your civilian clothes for storage." Then he called the squad leader, introduced me as a new addition, telling him to take care of everything else. With no hesitation, the squad leader, an average build sergeant, ordered me to follow him. We left the master sergeant's small office which was located in the corner of the barrack entrance, and entered a big open area furnished with two rows of bunk beds, neatly made with an isle in the middle. We stopped before the end of the barrack, he pointed at one of the upper bunk beds, telling me to use it. Then we went to the store-house, where I got a complete uniform set consisting of: a field shirt, breeches, forage cap, shoes, foot cloth, puttees, underwear and a towel. With all that gear, we left for the bath house.

We came back to the unit at supper time. The minute we entered the barrack we heard the voice of the soldier on duty announcing to get ready for supper and form in column. The squad leaders arranged the formation, and then the master sergeant led the company to the dining hall, which was big enough to accommodate the entire field engineer battalion. The number of personnel to be fed is submitted in advance to the dining hall manager. The sergeant on duty with the help of two soldiers receives the food and sets it up on the tables, each of which could seat ten soldiers, five on each side. We had for supper a bowl of pearl-barley porridge, two hundred grams of bread and tea. When we returned to the barracks, we had an hour of personal time for reading or writing letters, etc. The next routine was an evening check-up, a twenty minute evening walk, and then the sound of the bugle call, reminded us it's ten o'clock, time for retreat and to go to bed.

My Basic Training

The next day, at exactly six o'clock in the morning, I was woken up by the sound of the bugle and the loud voice of the soldier on duty, "reveille," amplified by the squad leaders who were woken up ten minutes earlier. We had three minutes to get dressed in a shirt, breeches, put on the foot cloth, shoes, the puttees (a cloth strip wrapped around the leg from ankle to knee) and get outside to line-up. From there, the squad leader led us for a twenty minute morning exercise which consisted of a short brisk walk, then running and calisthenics. After a wash-up in the wash-room, we returned to the barrack, made our beds, got fully dressed and went, organized in columns, for breakfast.

The remainder of the day went according to the schedule of the day, which included a briefing of the latest developments on the front, studying the regulations manual, an hour of exercises on a small gymnastic field outside in front of the barracks, equipped with parallel bars, high bar, rings and horse. After a substantial workout, we went for lunch, then siesta time, a mandatory one hour nap.

In the afternoon, we continued our study. This time it was parts and care of a rifle, the rest of the day went by routinely. The reveille of the next day was not so smooth as the first. While trying to get dressed on time, one of my puttees fell out of my hands and unrolled all over the floor. By the time I picked it up and put it back on, I was late for the line up so I was punished and drilled getting dressed and undressed repeatedly, then I had to catch up with the squad. I was not the only one late that morning; another soldier was too slow also, so when he got an order to hurry up he lashed out at the squad leader with profanities, saying "What's your hurry? Can't you wait another five or ten minutes?" The remaining personnel in the barracks exploded in laughter. The squad leader, stunned by the obvious earnestness of the situation, gave him a brief lecture on obedience and ordered him to catch up with the squad. The same soldier had another problem, namely a weak bladder he couldn't control. He urinated in his sleep, making his squad leader, who slept in the lower row of the same bunk, wet. All of these cases were reported to the platoon, company and commanding officers. As a result of a re-examination, that soldier was discharged from military service on the basis of mental and physical unfitness.

About two months went by at my basic training, during which we practiced parade, marching on drilling grounds, and started firing practice with rifles and machine guns. The rules and regulations for our company were strict, since the first company I was assigned to was a training company which prepares non-commissioned officers. I was the only Jew among our company personnel and no one knew it. I had a fair appearance with no Semitic traits.

On one of those days during a smoke break while practicing parade marching, I was standing with a friend not far away from our sergeant, an Ukranian, surrounded by a group of soldiers chatting about nationalities. I couldn't help but overhear one of his remarks, "All nationalities are okay, as long as they are not Jewish." It was very upsetting for me, but I managed to control my indignation and calmed down, realizing that, unfortunately, he was not the only one who thought that way. He was a person of small stature, with a light brown complexion and turned-up nose and a lower lip hanging over outward. When he spoke or issued commands, it was a mixture of Ukrainian and Russian that provoked a restrained laughter which apparently he didn't mind. But the outraged expression on my face didn't escape the attention of my friend. He called me aside telling me: "Why don't you change your name from Glick to Glickov, you will be much better off. Of course, this is only a suggestion and you'll have to make up your own mind." I expressed my thanks for his concern and advice, telling him that I am going to think about it and I did think a lot about it but my decision was not to change my family name.

He was a fair-dealing young man of average height, a descendant of the Russians who were exiled to Armenia in the 18th century by Catherine the Great, Empress of Russia, for their unorthodox beliefs. Their main occupation was farming. His mother used to come to visit him by train and bring some flat bread (lavash), cheese, dry fruits and tobacco which he sometimes shared with me. Only now it became clear to me why I saw only Russian draftees in the induction station. They were the young generation of the exiles. The other reason for that was the beginning of the creation of some segregated Armenian and Georgian units in that period of the war.

Winter was in full swing with a considerable amount of snow on the ground. On one of those cold days our squad went out to the shooting grounds for firing practice. Before we started to do the shooting, our sergeant gave us additional instructions on how to handle the rifle to be successful and quick in aiming and not miss the target. We started the drilling first with blanks. Apparently, I wasn't as quick as required, because he turned to me, telling me that I was slow, clumsy and was only pretending. He stopped the squad from practicing, and started to drill me alone, repeatedly commanding: "Hit the ground! On your feet! while the rest of the squad was waiting and trying to keep warm by jumping up and down and clapping their hands. As for me, I wasn't pretending. On the contrary, I was trying my best to do it quicker and better but I couldn't. The rifle with its bayonet was almost 1½ times my height, my hands and feet were cold, and I just didn't have the strength to do it fast enough. In the meantime, the waiting squad started to complain that they were cold but he didn't pay attention to their complaints and kept on ordering me to continue to practice. I couldn't anymore and started to cry. He lashed out, rebuking me and telling me about all the horrible conditions, adversities, sufferings and deaths on the front, "whereas we are in the rear in warm barracks, getting prepared and ready for replacements, whenever a need will arise for reinforcements, and we have to apply all our efforts to do so." He calmed down and ordered the squad to continue the drilling. Only when it became very windy, he stopped us, ordered us to form columns and return to the barracks.

About a week went by after these two incidents. The weather was still cold, but that didn't stop our routine training, this time with a newly appointed sergeant for our squad. The first one was transferred to an auxiliary platoon of our battalion for transportation and housekeeping. Apparently the incident during our training reached the headquarters. My suspicion was reinforced on the follow Sunday when I was approached by the senior sergeant for cultural affairs, who invited me to go with him to see a ballet, "Swan Lake," in the city of Erevan. I accepted the offer gladly. Later in the day we left by train for the city. It so happened that during the intermission, we met the chief engineer with his wife, from the company I worked for so briefly before my induction. He met us with the same smile as when we met the first time when he hired me to work for the company. We conversed for a while, then he invited us to the buffet for a small treat of pastry and soda, after which we went back to our seats.

We enjoyed the ballet very much, especially the music of Tchaikovsky. After the finale, we went back to the railroad station and returned to our unit late at night. Two days later in the early afternoon, I was called to the headquarters to the officer on duty, who told me that the deputy battalion commander wanted to see and that I should report to him right away. I straightened up my uniform, knocked on his door and entered his office, saluted, saying "Comrade Captain, I am reporting as ordered!" He invited me in and offered me a seat, telling me that he will be with me in a minute.

While he was busy with some papers, I looked him over. He was tall, impressive, with a firm but pleasant appearance, captain in rank. Shortly, he turned to me asking; "Comrade Glick, would you please tell me briefly, how you managed to escape alone at such a young age from the German onslaught." I did. He interrupted me, from time to time, asking for more details. When I finished, he asked me whether I enjoyed the ballet. I nodded, telling him "Very much so." He wished me good luck in the service and released me.

A week later a big article appeared in the local newspaper of our garrison, the author of which was none other than the captain, portraying me as an exemplary soldier, having some difficulties, not unusual for beginners, but trying his best.

Special Training

By the end of the month, we started classes in explosives, mines and their varieties, demolition with explosives, also introduction to pontoon types of temporary floating bridges and their assembly. Practice for these specialties was scheduled for summer time. A week later we were sent to dig trenches and work on other fortification installations not far away from the Turkish border. We worked there for about one month, marching to and from the place of work since our battalion had no means of transportation at that time, except horses and wagons. Every second day a freight train consisting of a small steam engine and two cars passed by on a nearby single railroad track, not clearly visible to us and stopped. We could not see what was going on, on the other side, loading or unloading. After a while, it returned in the direction that it came from. Apparently some kind of communication or quiet dealing took place and continued during our stay there. After all, Turkey was neutral during the war and tried to keep a low profile.

Other Assignments

In the early Spring, our company received a new assignment, blasting ice build-ups around piles of wooden bridges or frozen rivers in the vicinity of Stalingrad, to prevent damage or destruction by big chunks of cracked ice, driven by strong river currents, when the thaw would begin. We went by train, arrived in a place with bombed out buildings, which used to be a big junction and railway station, now in ruins, except for the restored railroad tracks. We got off the train and marched for a sizeable distance across a place full of rubble which used to be a big industrial and cultural center on the Volga river, the city of Stalingrad, now in ruins. What we witnessed was very distressing and a grim sight to look at, but unfortunately, real. We all experience a burst of indignation seeing the atrocious results committed by the German fascists, especially considering the countless innocent victims buried under the rubble.

Shortly we encountered a small structure that miraculously remained intact, where you could get hot, boiled water. We stopped there, had a snack by using our dry ration with a cup of hot boiled water. After a brief rest, we continued our march and left the limits of what used to be a city and entered a village with a frozen river and that was the first point of our destination. As usual, we found temporary accommodations in private dwellings. On the morning of the next day, we went out for a survey of the area. The ice was thick and the bridge frail. So our superiors decided to place small charges of explosives in dug-out holes on the ice, not too close to the piles, to avoid damage to the wooden structure of the bridge. We then set off the charges one by one. As a result, the solid ice cracked and was broken up in chunks, small pieces which would easily pass through the piles without causing any damage when the thaw set in. We accomplished our task safely and picked up a lot of stunned fish, which we gave to the housewives of our quarters, a very desirable treat, especially at that time.

We had one more bridge to take care of with a similar operation not far away downstream from the place we stayed which we also completed successfully and then returned to our unit, but not for long. About one week later our platoon received another order to leave for a special assignment to an undisclosed area. We barely managed to recover from the latest assignment, but nevertheless started to get ready for another one. One evening, we boarded a train, this time, not just our platoon but the entire company, and left. We arrived in a mountainous terrain with rocky rapids. We got an order to set up tents for a temporary stay. Our task was to start construction of wooden bridges capable of sustaining heavy equipment. Our company was divided into two groups and we started to work in two different places, not far from each other. We prepared construction stage areas for the delivery of equipment.

We managed to work there for a couple of weeks, and then our platoon only was recalled for another assignment. The other two platoons remained to complete the original construction job. We found out the details of our new task when we arrived in a dry steppe area, close to the Turkish border, which was to prepare, supervise and set off a blast for an irrigation canal. For that reason, the farmers of that area were mobilized to dig wells. We gave them instructions of the well dimensions and locations required: 4 feet in diameter, 10 feet deep, with a 4' – 4'6" recess at the bottom, located at a distance from each other, starting out in a straight line and then gradually forming a curve.

It took some time to complete the digging, after which we started to load explosives, mines and gun powder into the recesses, bringing out the wires from the detonators in wooden tubing to the surface and leaving them insulated. From that point on, we extended the wiring to a bunker, located at a considerable distance from the loaded wells, and handed the leads over to our commanding officer. The authorities on the canal project notified the local authorities, the border police and the Turkish government, that we are preparing a powerful blast for an irrigation canal close to their border. The note also included the date, the time of the projected blast with the advice to remove electrical and telephone poles in the areas affected, also to keep door and windows in nearby buildings open. Before the time of the scheduled blast, our platoon was assembled in a bunker built on an elevated site far away from the loaded wells. At the appointed time, the switch was turned on; the first thing that we felt was a very powerful, earth-shaking sensation, like a tremendous earthquake, followed by a very loud blast. We could hardly see anything while looking out through the small observation openings of the bunker. It was dark and dusty – what we did see were a lot of stones, small and big, flying sky high. It took quite a while for the dust and debris to settle down. Only then, we exited the bunker, so we could see almost the entire length of a huge "U" shaped, deep opening in the earth, starting out straight and gradually turning to a curve. The hard and dangerous work assigned to us was successfully completed. A few days later, we received an order to return to our base.

Surprise

One day, I was called to the office of the company commander. We had a brief general conversation during which he offered me a new position, namely, to start as a trainee to our battalion cooks. I agreed and was transferred to the housekeeping and transportation platoon. As a beginner, I observed and followed their activities all day. In the late afternoon, I went with them to receive provisions. A few weeks later, I was sent to our battalion medical unit for a check up and examination and I received an okay from the doctor and was then assigned to duty.

Everything was going ok and I liked my new assignment as well as the battalion personnel. From time to time, I even heard expressions of praise – but not for long. One afternoon, my turn for duty came, so I went to the dining hall and from there to the food storehouse with two soldiers on kitchen duty to receive provisions for the following day. After supper, I remained by myself in the kitchen. I familiarized myself with the menu of the day which was oatmeal porridge for breakfast, borsch (cabbage soup) with beef and pearl-barley porridge for dinner, and a ration of bread and millet porridge for supper. Breakfast and supper meals included tea and a ration of sugar and bread. After familiarizing myself with the menu, I started to prepare the meat by cutting it into small pieces, and there was plenty of cutting to do because I received a quarter of a cow to work with. It took me half a night to work on that. Then I started to prepare breakfast, oatmeal porridge for ordinary personnel and fried potatoes on the iron stove for officers.

When I was done with all that, I asked the stoker, to turn off the stove, which he did; then I removed the pan with the fried potatoes and stored it away. I still had some time to reveille, so I decided to wash my white uniform jackets. I hung them on a stirrer and a scoop with long wooden handles, which I placed on the cooled-off stove; then I sat nearby waiting for the sound of the bugle since I had everything ready for the morning breakfast. I made a big mistake doing that.

I was overworked from a very busy night duty. As a result, while sitting, I became drowsy and fell asleep not even realizing how and when.

Apparently the stoker stopped by and seeing me asleep, decided to play a "friendly" joke, although it was more an act of hate, namely, to turn on the stove again. I woke up to the sound of the bugle and the smell of smoke. The stove was red, the jackets in flames. I called the stoker right away and ordered him to turn the stove off. Then I opened the door wide to clear the area of the mess, smoke and steam created by extinguishing the fire from the items I removed carefully from the stove and dropped into a nearby sink, opening the cold water faucet. In the meantime, the officer on duty came in to the kitchen. I reported what happened to me while on duty. The soldier on kitchen duty also arrived. The officer ordered us to bring the area back to order and get ready to serve breakfast. That's what we did. The rest of the day went by normally. I served dinner and supper. A week went by and no disciplinary action was taken against me.

My New Assignment

One day, I was called to the office of the Chief of Staff. He offered me the opportunity to take courses designated for "Junior Electrical Specialists" in another city of the Union. It was an immediate opening and I had to decide right away. I agreed and left for that assignment the next week. Before leaving, I was approached by the newly appointed dining-hall manager, a master sergeant, with an offer to keep my present position as a cook. I declined it politely with no further explanation.

I arrived in my new destination as planned. I found out that it would be a speedy course for non-commissioned officers, where I would learn some basics of electricity and a variety of other specialties and practices. I stayed there for about four months and graduated with the rank of sergeant. Also for successful completion of the course, I was awarded three weeks of furlough, which I used after my return to the unit. Our battalion commander congratulated me and approved my award. I was given three weeks of leave and left right away for my birthplace, a small town Sniatyn, on the Polish-Romanian border, located in the southwest of what was then Poland and is now the Ukraine.

Close to the end of the war, when the territory I lived in was liberated, I started to communicate with the town authorities, numerous times, to find out what happened to my family, but I never got a response. It became clear to me that no one remained alive. But still, I wanted to find out personally what happened from the authorities or neighbors. I arrived in the town early in the morning and walked along empty streets, not a living soul around; until I entered the center and introduced myself as a native of this town to the first person I met, since I was wearing a military uniform. He gave me an address of the person I should go and see. I did so, and to my surprise, we knew each other and, not only that, he was also a business partner of my brother-in-law who had a barber shop. It so happened that my brother-in-law was drafted into the army when the war started. Later on, he was released from service because of an illness and was sent away to the rear of the country. When our town was liberated, he returned and continued to work as a barber again. His first wife, who was one of my sisters, shared the same fate as the rest of my family; they were all brutally killed, except one of my older brothers who was drafted before the war and myself, by managing to run away to the rear of the country. Both of us were the lucky ones who remained alive.

In the afternoon, I went to see the area where our house, shop and street used to be. All of that had disappeared. It was a distressful and painful view. I managed to control myself but not completely. Streams of tears kept pouring from my eyes continuously. After a while, I forced myself to calm down because I had expected to encounter a situation like this. I then decided to stop by in the house of one of my Christian neighbor's which was still intact and only a street away to find out whether or not she can or would give me some details of what happened. Her name was Frania Bordun. This is what she told me. All of the Jews were locked up in a ghetto created in town, forbidden to exit or leave it to work, shop or anything else. After a short while, the killings started. The sick ones were shot in their beds (among them one of my older sisters who was paralyzed). Most of the rest were shot in a nearby forest "Potoczek" on the outskirts of the town, and some were taken away by freight cars from the nearby railroad station Sniatyn-Zalucze, three or four kilometers way, to the death camps. I left her house even more distressed from what I heard but again had to control myself.

I went back to the house of my ex- brother-in-law deciding to cut short my leave but both he and his wife insisted and talked me into staying with them for the rest of my furlough. It was nice and generous of them, especially in those days. I agreed and was very thankful for that. I was treated as a family member, exceptionally warm, with sincere compassion. Before I left, my brother in law told me that he would convey the good news to my brother who was in New York and with whom he communicated, since I could not, that I was alive and well on active duty in the Russian army.

Return to my Stationed Unit

I reported back to my Unit. Shortly thereafter, I was assigned to our engineering platoon at the rank of a squad leader of our mobile electrical unit, which consisted of two trucks, one with a generator that provided field lighting and another one with electrical construction tools. My service in my new position continued with a variety of new assignments. On one of the first days, the company master sergeant ordered me to lead our platoon for the morning exercise, which I did. What I noticed and heard, while pronouncing my commands, was a restrained laughter, because I spoke with a burr. In America and in many other countries of the world, to speak with a burr is a normal, conventional occurrence in speech and even considered pleasant in a lot of countries, but not in Russia. That's why I firmly decided to get rid of it. I knew that it would not be easy. I also realized that the only way to achieve that goal was to continuously practice my pronunciation with my tongue and not my throat. I started to do so right away, quietly, while sitting or walking, so no one, if present, could hear it. I kept on constantly repeating words and familiar proverbs containing the letter "r" pronouncing it with my tongue. Eventually, I succeeded. The next time I lined up the squad or platoon for that matter, to lead them for exercises, I pronounced the letter "r" in a prolonged a clear way, without burring, while giving the commands. The troops were pleasantly surprised and even shocked for a moment, and then I received loud applause and praise for my will power and success in achieving my goal.

The war was over. I hoped that shortly I would be demobilized but that did not happen. The international situation worsened at that time and became very tense. I stopped thinking of an early discharge completely and my service continued in its normal routine. Shortly, I received a new assignment to provide lighting in temporary summer camps for officers to exercise and practice mountaineering in some places in the Caucasian mountains. I left there with one of my squad soldiers in a special truck equipped with a powerful mobile electrical generator and the required specialized equipment for temporary camp lighting.

We arrived there at the beginning of summer. We settled down in a clear, open grassy area at the foot of the high, steep mountains, covered with white glittering snow, most of it on its peaks –so bright, one could not look at it without sunglasses. Then we installed a tent with provisions for summer camping, parked our truck not too far away, removed and fortified the mobile generator to the ground, removed the lighting equipment and placed it nearby for readiness.

The entire area and the particular spot we settled down in, was very beautiful. The area all around was a highland district, with variable breeds of tall dense trees, mountain streams, loudly rippling and flowing endlessly. In a few locations in the same area were medicinal mineral waters flowing from small pipes installed on the rocky ground.

Shortly, an infantry platoon from another unit arrived with an assignment to provide all required services for the mountaineers. The first thing they did was the installation of tents for the arriving officers from some military districts of the Union, and for themselves. Afterwards, we started to install lighting in the tents and two wooden structures. Since the two of us were not entitled to the same quality of food as the officers, we were assigned to the infantry platoon for food provisions. We stayed with the mountaineers to the end of summer, providing the service required from us completely without problems, and then we returned to our unit.

A few months after my return to my Unit, I received a letter in an unsealed envelope from my ex-brother-in-law. In it was enclosed a small letter sent to me by my brother from New York City, stating that he was very happy and rejoiced at the good news conveyed to him that I was alive, well and still on active duty in the Russian Army. He also informed me that his wife was a native of the Ukraine, from the city of Kremenchug, and that her parents still live there. He also gave me their address and advised me to start to communicate with them. I did do so.

In the meantime my service continued with the same everyday routine. Three more summers in a row. I got the same assignment to stay with the mountaineers and provide lighting for their camps in the same area and on the same spot. A year later, in springtime, an order was issued to discharge servicemen by their year of birth, which I was subject to. This time I had to make up my mind where to go? There was a law providing choices all over the country, with some restrictions. I firmly decided not to return to the town of my birth, it would be painful and offer no future. So, I thought that, for a start, it would be a good idea to choose the city of Kremenchug, where the in-laws of my brother lived. My decision was also based on the fact that while communicating with them during my remaining service time, I was always reminded that I was welcome to come and stay with them after demobilization, until I settle down. So I handed in my application to staff headquarters requesting to make out my discharge documents and travel tickets to that city.

Back to Civilian Life

It took me two days of travel by train to arrive at the city of my destination. I arrived there late in the morning and got information about the location of the place I had to go to from a militiaman on duty outside of the half-destroyed railway station. Then, I picked up my suitcase with the kit-bag and left, walking slowly with frequent stops, observing the surrounding streets with destroyed housing or empty sites. An embracing quietness existed all around; there was almost no street traffic. One could hear from time to time the sound of the train siren and its movement of the railway system not far away. Finally, I approached the house where my brother's in-laws lived. It was a small, one-story building with a few apartments, common corridor, backyard and an outdoor toilet facility. I was warmly welcomed while entering their apartment which consisted of one room and a small kitchen for four people: husband and wife, daughter and four year old son. I realized right away that my stay with them would have to be as brief as possible, taking into account their living conditions. Of course, I was treated nicely and cordially but nevertheless I decided to try vigorously to find employment, rent a room or a corner for that matter, in a more suitable place. In the meantime, while staying there, I used a folding bed in a corner of the room to sleep on. I knew that housing was not going to be easy to find; new construction was very slow, almost at a standstill. A short time afterwards, a friend of my relatives offered me help in getting a job in a printing shop. He worked there and knew someone in the management. He was successful and I got a job. My starting time was the first of the week. I was very happy and excited.

Any beginning of employment was very important for my immediate needs, to start to build a self supporting life. I had managed to work just a few days when my relatives began to talk about marriage, starting right away with a proposal to marry their daughter. It was no surprise or shock to me, I expected that and had a definite, ready answer, but tried to be nice and polite. My reply was as follows: I was young, still only at the start and not sure of steady employment, and barely able to support myself in the present situation. Their daughter, much older than I was, had no skill or profession, a divorcee with a four year old son and not attractive to me. I felt sorry for them but that was the case – she was no match for me.

They didn't like my decision but I couldn't do otherwise. From that day on, I started to search and inquire for another place to stay. I didn't have to go too far. When one of my co-workers found out that I was searching for a place to live, he offered me a place in his house where he lived with only his mother. I agreed, as a temporary measure, and moved into the new place. I didn't expect such a quick solution but was happy that I found another "corner" to stay. In the meanwhile, I started to familiarize myself with the city and made new friends. Somehow I caught a cold and went to see a doctor. I also asked him to give me a general check-up. He did and told me that I was in good shape, physically fit but a little bit under stress and that I had to control that. He gave me two prescriptions, one for a cold and the other to relieve the stress.

The city had two drugstores. I went to the central one to get the prescriptions filled. Still, I had to stand in a long line and wait for my turn. When I got to the half-glazed counter with a small window, I saw a nice young lady pharmacist with a very pleasant appearance, beautiful eyes and attractive smile. It was love from the first sight. What I had to find out is whether she is married or free. I handed over my prescriptions, she looked at them, then at me, telling me that I'd have to wait for the prescriptions and come back in a few hours to receive them. Pharmacies in those days operated twenty-four hours a day, seven days a week. I also found out that she worked till nine in the evening, then the place closed, except for an on-duty pharmacist who stays there for emergency service only. When I came back for my medicine, she asked me whether or not I was new in this city, since I still wore my military uniform, without shoulder straps. I confirmed that I was new and saying good-night, left.

A week later after a partial recovery, I had a strong desire to see her again. So I went there approximately before the end of the work day and strolled alongside the drugstore. A while later I could see her through the window without the uniform, getting ready to go home. When she came out, I approached and greeted her, asking permission to walk alongside her, since I have to go in the same direction. I noticed that she was pleasantly surprised and agreed. So we left walking slowly, telling each other stories about our lives. The time went by so quickly that we did not notice that we approached her house. Before saying goodnight, I thanked her for allowing me to walk her home, telling her how much I had enjoyed talking to her. I also asked her to allow me to see her again sometime, saying I would appreciate it very much. I got a positive answer. On that note, I thanked her and, saying goodnight, left.

One day, while being outdoors with friends, I stopped by the drugstore to see her and say hello to my new acquaintance, Miss Sofia. She was not in that day. One of the pharmacists informed me that she was working the day shift that week, nine to three. Since I was working till five o'clock, I decided to see her the following week. In the meantime, some fellows I had met tried to introduce me to a number of young girls because, in these post-war times, the shortage and demand for men was critical. But I refused to make any new acquaintances and I had firmly decided to go steady with Sofia, since, when I asked her if she was seeing someone, her answer was no. We met a few more times in the evenings after work. On one of those evenings, she invited me for the next Sunday to meet and have dinner with her parents. I gladly accepted the invitation, met the parents and the rest of the family as planned, got well acquainted with them. I briefly told them some of my life story and had an enjoyable dinner with them. All of them were polite, warm and friendly. I didn't have such a good dinner since I left my brother-in-law's house.

In the meantime, my temporary living in the house of my co-worker didn't work out as I expected. While paying them almost all my salary for nourishment and lodging, I was half-hungry all the time. Since I had no other choice, I had to take it as it was. I kept on dating Sofia accompanying her often from work on her way home. A few times we went to the movies; ticket prices in those days had become very inexpensive. I found out that she liked to dance and so did I. The city also had an area in the park set off for dancing, so I invited her to a dance party and we both enjoyed it and had a very good time. While walking her home, I told her that I liked her very much and shared with her my thoughts about marriage, asking her whether she would agree to marry me. She responded that she also liked me but still wanted to think about it and talk to her family to listen to their opinion, and then she would let me know her decision.

We met again on a Sunday, went for a walk to a nearby botanical garden. While walking slowly and enjoying the smell of the flowers and fresh air, we engaged ourselves in an intimate talk, discussing a variety of subjects, including my present situation. She gave me the good news first, saying that she decided to accept my proposal and agrees to marry me. We embraced and kissed each other passionately. We continued our walk, and then sat down for a while on a bench.

Afterwards, I walked her home. Before saying goodbye to each other, she told me that her parents had invited me to their home for lunch the following Sunday. I gladly accepted the invitation.

This was only my second visit to her family and it was very desirable and exciting. We enjoyed lunch together, after which her mother and father told us that they would not stand in the way of getting married, and that they were very happy to see that we like each other and that they would arrange, prepare and organize a wedding party for us as soon as possible. In those days, there were no wedding halls in the city or restaurants so they decided to do it in their apartment house which also had a large back yard. Since private telephones were a rarity for most people, except for a few officials, and for a few of the well-to-do, they decided to notify and invite relatives and friends in person. Her parents also proposed to give us, after the wedding, a room in their apartment, temporarily until we could find and rent one ourselves.

We had our wedding ceremony performed in a civil registrar's office, then a very lovely dinner reception in their house. I was delighted and surprised to see serving tables covered the white table-cloths, plentiful appetizers, beverages, soft-drinks, liquor, vodka and wine. You could also sense the pleasant smell of meals cooked and warming in preparation to be served.

All the rooms were fully packed with relatives and friends. An accordionist was playing cheerful melodies and all of us had a very good time.

I have to admit that both her mother and father were very sensible, decent and honest people. I was very luck to become a member of their family. In that time, the struggle for a livelihood was a very difficult one. Her parents deserve a lot of credit for the way they organized and prepared the wedding party under the circumstances. It is still hard to understand how they managed to arrange all of that, especially her mother, considering the difficult living conditions that then existed. It was a hot summer, and they had neither a refrigerator nor air-conditioning. Later I found out that they had borrowed the money they needed for the wedding from relatives and friends and that it took then a long time to pay off the loans.

I left my co-workers house and moved in with my in-laws in a separate room given to us temporarily after the wedding. We were both very happy, especially I, starting our new married life in a good atmosphere and reasonably good conditions. Soon, my wife persistently urged me to continue my education which was interrupted by the war. I listened to her and signed up for evening classes to get a high school diploma. A year later I graduated and took up correspondence courses in a technical school. In the meantime, I maintained my correspondence with my brother and let him know that I got acquainted and fell in love with a beautiful young girl from a very nice family. She, a pharmacist by profession, worked in a city pharmacy as an assistant manager. He congratulated us, wishing we well and sent a big parcel with clothing for both of us as a wedding present.

Nine months later my wife gave birth to a beautiful son who we named Joseph in honor of my late father. We also tried to start searching for an apartment, since we had a new addition to our family but her parents stopped us insisting that it is too early to look for a separate apartment, considering our needs at the time: both working, taking care of the newborn, and the extreme shortage of apartments caused by wartime destruction.

Our life proceeded with the accustomed after-war difficulties but we somehow managed. Another year and a half went by. My wife gave birth to another beautiful son, we named him Boris. This time we started to search vigorously for a badly needed apartment. The only place we found one was on the outskirts of the town, a bungalow in the backyard of a privately owned house. We rented it and moved in. From that moment on, my mother-in-law used to come to us by bus and baby sit for our children. She was a very pleasant and loyal lady, like my own mother used to be, let her rest in peace. A lot of married couples dreamed to have such mothers.

`

The Apartment

In the meantime, a four-story housing unit built by one of the city factories was in the completion stage. Since the place I worked in was a part of the factory, I applied for an apartment. It took me a lot of work and many petitions to the authorities to apply for that apartment but it was worth it and not in vain. They granted a room for my family in a three room apartment with central heating, common kitchen and bathroom. The other two rooms were assigned to another couple with two children and a mother. The location of the apartment was on the first floor. The move was scheduled to take place on the evening of the New Year. It was a very happy evening for all of us, not only because we got a chance to move out from that wet bungalow which was an unhealthy place to live in, especially for the two small children, but it was also a chance to move into a brand new apartment room still with the smell of fresh paint. The other good thing about it was the location of the building which was very close to the place we both worked. We also realized that it was going to be tight living quarters but we were very happy with it and we saw it like a happy dream come true, considering the after-war housing shortage.

But things turned around in a very ugly way, temporarily spoiling our happiness and excitement; when my family and myself arrived at the building to move in, we found out that the room designated for us, was illegally occupied by someone else. It was a shock to all of us, especially to me, but I calmed down, kept on controlling myself and the family and so decided to stay with the family in the corridor, not far away from the entrance until someone from the authorities would solve the problem, since we were the legally approved tenants of that room. While sitting on the packs in the corridor, settled in tenants and guests entered and left the corridor, walking up and down the stairs, since elevators had not been planned for this building, staring at us compassionately. We also heard the sounds of festive New Year's music as the apartment doors opened and closed. Shortly, a representative from the authorities with two militiamen showed up and tried to talk to, and convince, the violators to get out and leave the premises and building, but in vain, they refused. It was almost midnight when the superintendant showed up telling us that he would move us temporarily into a typical apartment room on the fourth floor until the problem was resolved. He also stated that it would not take long to move us back into our designated apartment room on the first floor. With that, he asked us to follow him to the new place. We did so, and moved in. Before he left, we expressed our gratitude and wished him a very happy and healthy New Year. He reciprocated wishing us the same and left. A couple of weeks later, the authorities notified us that our legally designated room was free to move into. We did so, slowly and happily. We bought some new furniture on credit and enjoyed our new common apartment.

Shortly, a very unusual, strange and sinister occurrence took place in the city, and that was a torchlight procession on one of the evenings. A very long, formed column of people paraded on the main street of the city toward the end of it, extinguishing and throwing the torches away on an empty square. What remained of that event were a very bad smell of left-over smoke in the air and a feeling of disgust and disappointment. An event like that could not have happened without the knowledge and approval of the city authorities, or it could have been some kind of test.

Things kept on passing by quietly and normally. One morning, while going to work and walking by a newsstand, my attention turned to a very hard, strange and unbelievable headline which appeared all of a sudden in the official newspaper, Pravda (Truth) about a conspiracy by a group of doctors. I bought the paper and continued to walk until I entered my place of work. Since I was early and still had some time to read it, I did so and was astounded reading it, so I reread it again and stopped – it was time to start work. I did so, but my mind was disturbed. All of a sudden, a leading editorial of that paper was accusing some Moscow doctors, with Jewish surnames, of a conspiracy to kill Soviet leaders. The news spread instantly. One could hear and feel it, right away all around you with a variety of anti-Semitic derogatory expressions. You could also hear a little bit later, disturbing threats and rumors that empty freight cars were ready and waiting at the freight yard of the railway.

What really happened, only someone high up in authority would know but apparently some very responsible and authoritative leaders realized that this was a dangerous and unprecedented situation and that an untrue accusation could nevertheless cause catastrophic consequences. The general feeling and mood created a tense and hateful mind in those reading the article. Luckily and very shortly afterwards, another leading editorial of the same appeared again with the following headline: "Soviet Justice is Inviolable" acknowledging that all accusations were a big mistake, untrue and fake. But the after-effects of that sudden false accusation remained in some minds for a while but slowly and eventually was forgotten, but, apparently, not by everybody. The hatred instigated and left over by the German fascist occupiers and their local collaborators, which still existed, hidden, was exposed.

Repatriation

In the meantime, an agreement was concluded and signed between the then Soviet Union and the Polish government for the repatriation of former Polish citizens, including Jewish nationals, who were born and lived there until 1939, before the Second World War.

Since I managed to escape and saved myself from the brutal, murderous hands of the German Nazis and their local collaborators, remaining the only survivor, apart from an older brother who also managed to survive and lived with his family in New York City, out of a family of thirteen: my Father, Mother, my Grandmother, four brothers, six sisters and also a number of relatives, I decided to apply to the local authorities as a start to petition for an exit visa for me and my family to be repatriated to Poland on the basis of the newly concluded agreements between the two governments.

I did so, and went there in person, expressed my request orally, which was ridiculed and rejected off-hand. Then I started to petition higher authorities, by travelling once to Kiev and six times to Moscow, and still did not get my response. During this time, while awaiting an approval to my request, my shop superintendant approached me while working telling me to hand in my application for a voluntary "resignation." from my job. I refused, understandably. Subsequently, I made another attempt, the seventh and last, travelling to Moscow again to see higher authorities and to ask them once again to approve my request. I also went to the Polish Consulate and met with one of their representatives who promised me that he would intervene on my behalf and help me. While there, I also went shopping and bought some clothing for the children, a commodity which was more easily accessible in Moscow than in smaller, regional cities. Then I left home by train.

About a week later I received a telephone call at work from the local authorities who had handled my case, telling me that my request was approved and that I should come in to their office to select a point of exit to Poland. I did so and selected the city of Brest, located on the west side of the Soviet-Polish border. I was also informed that I have two weeks' time to arrange our departure which was more than enough, and that I was entitled to an exchange of all our State Loan bonds for cash, since we were leaving the country on a permanent basis. We cashed the bonds, it was not much but it was very helpful. We rented a container, packed our belongings and sent them away by freight to remain in Poland, to the city of Wroclow (Breslau) till claimed by its owners.

During these two weeks, and before that, numerous attempts were made by acquaintances of my wife to persuade her not to go with me but to leave me instead. Also, her parents were persuaded to encourage her to stay, because if she left, there would be no chance of return. But she firmly stood by her decision to go with me. One evening later, my wife, myself and our two sons, accompanied by my Mother and Father-in-law, a number of relatives, friends and acquaintances, escorted us to the train to say goodbye. It was a very emotional moment for all of us, with hugging, kissing and crying.

Very shortly, we heard the warning siren of our train for boarding so we did, talking up our assigned seats in a compartment of a sleeping car. Soon we felt a slight jolt, and the train started out on the journey at a slow speed, eventually increasing to a normal one. Our eyes followed those accompanying us, waving our hands through the open windows, so did they, reciprocating with good wishes, until we couldn't see each other anymore.

The monotonous rumble and knock of the train wheels made us sleepy. We were awakened by the conductor in the morning when we arrived and entered the border City of Brest. Shortly, the frontier guards showed up checked our documents and exit visas. We got off the train, one official met and welcomed us, and then he escorted us to a temporary place set up for repatriates. We remained there for a few days, and then we left westwards to the district city of Wroclaw. While there, we found out that some relatives of mine and landsmen live in the city of Legnica, which was not far away. So we decided to go there, take up our first residence and settle down. We were warmly met by friends we knew before and relatives who rendered their assistance to us by offering us a temporary stay in one of the rooms of their apartment until we get one from the City, as new repatriates. It was a very generous and friendly gesture.

We moved in and subsequently applied to the authorities for an apartment which we got after a brief wait. To begin with, we started to buy some basic living necessities. Our next need was for employment, so my wife, a pharmacist by profession, started first to search for employment. She applied to the district office of the region with a request for work which was approved. She got a position in her field in one of the local pharmacies in Legnica. So we decided that I would take care of the children temporarily until I found a job. We managed to register our older son in school which he started to attend. We also contacted my brother and relatives in New York, who urgently advised us to get registered at the American Embassy in Warsaw and to get on the list for emigration to the USA. While there, the person we were interviewed by informed us that we couldn't emigrate all together at the same time. At that time, the law allowed only the head of the family to enter the country, find employment and only then, would he get permission to bring over the rest of his family. It was a little bit upsetting in the beginning but we overcame it. Very shortly, the Congress in the USA approved and passed a resolution not to separate families but let them emigrate all together. In fact, we received a letter form an office of the U.S. consulate in Warsaw, notifying us about that decision. It was encouraging and very good news which made us all very happy. Apparently someone prayed very hard for us.

Subsequently my brother let us know that he and our relatives had hired a lawyer to make out and prepare an affidavit of support for all of us. In the meantime, we continued our normal life, working and taking care of the children, getting some financial help from my brother and relatives. We also established an acquaintance with some other people who were registered for emigration. At the beginning of summer, we received a letter from the American Consulate with a note to appear for an interview; we did so, and while there, we experienced a very positive and pleasant atmosphere. We also took a medical examination by assigned physicians who found us all to be in good health. A while later, we received one more letter from the Consulate in Warsaw which said that all of us, together, had been given permission to enter the U.S.A. We decided to sail on a passenger-ship which was preferable to my wife, rather than by air. So my brother bought the tickets for us on a Polish Ocean liner "Batory" which sailed and landed in the Canadian port of Montreal. From there we boarded a train for New York, the point of our destination. We had to use that route since, in the sixties, Polish ships did not have permission to enter American seaports.

We had stayed in Poland, the city of Legnica, for two years and left by train to the seaport of Gdynia, located in the northern part of Poland, on the Baltic sea, in the beginning of November 1960.

I recall some very strange and curious events which happened to us during our stay there which I would also like to mention. A few weeks before we left the city, I went to pick up my wife from work. When I approached the pharmacy, a heavy-set individual grabbed me from behind putting his hands around me and holding me very strongly, as if by pincers, and not letting me go. I tried to free myself but in vain. I decided also not to engage him in a fight. I was no match for him. I knew he had something on his mind to do, just to prevent our departure, but changed his mind and intentions at the last minute and released me, without saying anything and disappeared. Soon, my wife came out and we went home safely. The other occurrence I recall is the case on the train to the seaport of Gdynia. One evening the four us boarded sleeping compartments and left the city of Legnica, heading to the seaport of our intended departure. We barely managed to settle ourselves in when suddenly we heard a knock on the door of our compartment. I opened it. The face of an unknown man appeared with another one who let him into the compartment and, without saying a work, closed the door behind him and disappeared. We noticed that the man had a scar across his right cheek, with an ironical expression and a disturbing grimace which was supposed to be a friendly smile. He greeted us, stretched out his hand toward me, shook hands, then patted the boys heads and turning to me started bragging with no pause for questions: "We took them out, started to shoot them down, with submachine guns, they started to scatter around, trying to escape , disperse and hide but there was no place to do so. In any case, we got them all and no one managed to get out alive." While listening to his disgusting bragging, which was outrageous but unfortunately true, I felt that this was meant to entrap me and did not let him, or the thugs who sent him, achieve his goal, which was to disrupt my balance and engage me in a scuffle which would delay or prevent my departure. Fortunately, he did not obtain his desire, so abruptly left our compartment and disappeared.

We all went to sleep after that, tired of listening to his disgusting speech. As for me, it took me a while to calm down but I tried very hard and eventually I succeeded and also fell asleep. We woke up in the morning and eventually arrived in the seaport of Gdynia where the ocean liner was moored. Before we got off the train, frontier guards double-checked our documents and exit visas, found everything in order and then let us get off. We boarded the liner in the afternoon and left the coastline of Poland the same day. It took us ten days of sailing out of which nine were pleasant, with small exceptions which usually occur on a ship to some passengers such as dizziness and vomiting. The kids and myself had no problem, except my wife who had to stay in bed almost all the time because she felt dizzy and weak. On the tenth day of our voyage while the ship was approaching the shores of Canada, we were hit by a gale storm and woken up in the middle of the night. The ship was in disarray, turning in circles, our bodies being tossed up and down in our beds. It was very scary. Fortunately, we had a very courageous and skillful crew that managed to save us and the ship from that storm. What we found out in the morning was that the cable of the rudder had broken and was repaired thanks to the skilful divers who dived under the ship in spite of the storm, and fixed the rudder and successfully solved the problem. The crew had readied the life-boats but luckily there was no need for that. In the morning, the storm, slowly but surely faded away. When we entered the port of Montreal, the water was calm and the ship was moored. We disembarked and went ashore. In the evening of the same day, we boarded a train for New York. That was the last leg of our destination. While on the train, American authorities interrogated us, checked our documents, found everything in order and with wishes of good luck gave us the okay to continue our trip safely. All of us were very happy and excited.

Our Final Destination – The United States of America

We arrived in the morning in Grand Central Station, in New York City, met with a joyful welcome by my relatives, my late brother Morris, my cousin Louis who took us in his station wagon to an apartment which had been rented for us, close to the place he used to reside with his family. I had a very generous and loyal brother, also family and landsmen who helped us a lot upon our arrival and later on, starting us out with packed kitchen cabinets and refrigerator with food stuffs. They also provided us with some furnishings, dishes and other basic necessities.

Soon, I signed up for and attended free English language evening classes for beginners at the local high school and vigorously started to search for employment. Thus, we were getting ready to have a new beginning in our lives with excitement and hope.

About a month went by since we settled down in the City of New York. Thanks to the help of my late brother and his friends, I got a promise of a prospective job. To get there, I had to use the subway system, which was walking distance from the apartment building in which we lived. I also got directions about how to get there. By that time, I had already become a bit familiarized with it. On an early Monday morning, I got up and dressed. We had no radio or T.V. set at that time to listen to the weather forecast, and if we had, I am doubtful that we would have understood what they were saying anyway. I did not look out from the windows and dressed lightly and went outside to go to work. But I was surprised by an unexpected change in the weather, namely a heavy and deep snowfall, high above the knees, which happened overnight and which was something not new to me. No snow removal had started yet and it was even difficult to open the vestibule door. Most transportation was at a standstill. It was unusually quiet outside. From time to time, I could hear the rumble of wheels from the subway trains that were running but very slowly. I was undecided about what to do – to keep my job appointment or not – would the place be opened or closed.

I was too superstitious not to go, since this was my first attempt to get a job and not to fulfill it would be a bad sign, so I decide to go and did so. It took me quite a while just to get to the station and then to wait for the next train, which eventually came. I entered it with a great sense of relief. It took the train some time to get there and I found the place locked. I was disappointed but still hopeful and returned home late in the afternoon. A little while later, I got the job and was very glad and happy that, from now one, we were going to live in this beautiful country. Eventually, we all became citizens of the United States of America.

End

Made in the USA
Lexington, KY
28 October 2013